The great Coffee book

The great Coffee book

Timothy J. Castle and
Joan Nielsen

TEN SPEED PRESS
BERKELEY   TORONTO

We dedicate this book, with love, to each other.

🔟 Ten Speed Press
P.O. Box 7123
Berkeley, California 94107
www.tenspeed.com

Distributed in Australia by Simon and Schuster Australia, in Canada by Ten Speed Press Canada, in New Zealand by Southern Publishers Group, in South Africa by Real Books, and in the United Kingdom and Europe by Airlift Books.

The publisher would like to thank the following photographers for permission to use their work in this book:
Anacafe/Dario Morales: 2; 16; 30; 43
The <www.estatecafe.com> Archive: 14 (inset); 28; 46 (top and bottom); 48 (top and inset); 49
Jane Armstrong: 101; 105
Richard Phillip Brown: vi; 9; 21; 26; 79; 80; 81; 82; 99; 112; 114; 116; 127; 131; 136; 144; 147
Timothy Castle: 37
Frankie Frankeny: front cover; ii, 71
Craig Harrold: 59; 62-63; 67
Russell Kramer:3; 4
James Marcotte: 6-7; 10-11; 13; 32 (top, center, and bottom); back cover
Sherri Miller: 14 (top); 36; 40; 41; 44; 50; 51 (top and bottom); 53; 60; 84; 86; 93
Joan Nielsen: 8; 12; 68 (top and bottom); 73; 110; 115; 123; 134; 139 (top and bottom); and food styling: 112; 114; 116; 127; 131; 136; 144; 147
PhotoDisc: spine; viii; 64; 103
Melissa Pugash: 34
Tony Stone: 106

"Q&A" features that appear in this book were adapted from Timothy J. Castle's "Ask the Expert" column, in the short-lived but brilliant magazine, *The Coffee Journal*.

Design by Catherine Jacobes Design, San Francisco

Library of Congress Cataloging-in-Publication Data
Castle, Timothy James.
    The great coffee book / Timothy J. Castle and Joan Nielsen.
        p. cm.
Includes index.
ISBN 1-58008-122-3 (pbk.)
    1. Coffee. 2. Cookery (Coffee) I. Nielsen, Joan. II. Title.
TX583.C37 1999
641.3'373--dc21

                                   99-050069

First printing 1999
Printed in Hong Kong
2 3 4 5 6 7 8 9 10 — 09 08 07 06 05 04

Contents

ACKNOWLEDGMENTS

From Tim: The idea for this book, a concise, straightforward, and opinionated volume about a wonderful and simple thing—a great cup of coffee—was my co-author's. Joan Nielsen also supplied the perseverance, professionalism, and  skills (both literary and culinary) at every step. I owe my chief acknowledgment, if that word can encompass the gratitude and appreciation I feel, to her. And so, I raise a toast of freshly brewed, inky strong, deeply aromatic coffee to Joan!

Long overdue recognition goes to two of my earliest teachers. Alfred Peet provided my primary education in the appreciation of coffee, through its rigorous organoleptic evaluation (known as "cupping" and described herein). Carlernst Diedrich shared what coffee can be, and helped me understand what it has been. I thank them both for their generosity of time and spirit.

I'm grateful to the very special coffee farmers I've worked with over the years. Without their coffee I would have little to talk about: Bill McAlpin and Carole Kurtz of Costa Rica; the Janson family of Panama; the Eduardo deAndrade family of Brazil; and the Dieseldorffs of Guatemala. Thanks for the great coffee!

My appreciation also goes to Kevin Knox, a colleague and a fellow coffee book author. His wit, intelligence, and unflinching honesty are a constant source of inspiration. For almost twenty years now, I've felt blessed to share my ongoing coffee education with several uncommonly intelligent and warm-hearted people. I hope they won't mind if I refer to them as friends and colleagues: Paul Leighton, Carlo DiRuocco, Jane McCabe, Tim McCormack, Jim Reynolds, and Sam Schank. Thanks to many others who've helped me with articles and interviews over the years: Jerry Baldwin, Don Holly, Jay Isais, Klaus Monkemueller, Jon Stefenson, Roland Veit, and Jeremy Woods. My friendship with Wendy Rasmussen and Rick Rhinehart, two eminent coffee and tea professionals, is one that I cherish and always will.

Finally, I would like to thank my sister, Pam Stillings, and my father, Alex Castle, who've had to deal with an exceptionally distracted associate during the writing of this book. Space and common sense prohibit me from listing my customers and clients by name, but thanks to them all, nonetheless.

From Joan: When I first met Timothy Castle, he was a keynote speaker at a coffee conference. His speech vibrated with such knowledge, passion, and devotion, that I was left with the sense of having heard a master (and with an aspiration to work with him). Now, this goal has been realized. I've always loved coffee—chugging it strong and black, savoring (gasp!) those dreadful coffee-flavored milk drinks, sipping benign decaf. But I only learned a true appreciation of the bean through Tim. So here's to that (sweet) coffee curmudgeon and the drink that brought us together!

I give humble thanks to my teachers. I'll never forget Wolfgang Puck's classes and the week of lessons with the very funny Julia Child. And thanks to all those wonderful cooks and writers who've encouraged and inspired me: Marion Cunningham, Diana Kennedy, Julie Sahni, and Paula Wolfert, to name a few. But, by far the most important and inspiring person is my best friend, Helen Nielsen Allen. She's been the standard of excellence in this life of food I've chosen. Her testing of often impossible recipes and attention to grammatical detail are just two of the many unpaid jobs that she willingly performs for me. Thank you, Mother.

Acknowledgments would not be complete without mentioning the champions of this book. Most of the visuals come from the generous hearts and talented eyes of our good friends from around the world. First, a mighty thank you to Richard Brown of Los Angeles, for his excellent shots of food and coffee paraphernalia. Sherri Miller of Allegro Coffee, Denver, gave us her evocative photos that speak volumes about the world of coffee. Kai Janson of Café Volcán Barú, Panama; Russell Kramer of Hacienda La Minita, Costa Rica; and Anacafe of Guatemala contributed beautiful photos of the bean—its growth, harvesting, and processing. The old sepia photos of coffee farming and its peoples were lent from the collection of James Marcotte, Los Angeles. The antique coffee cards come through the generosity of my notable card-collecting father, William S. Nielsen, Sr., Cape Cod. Thank you, all. Finally, a very special thanks goes to a true coffee aficionado, Christopher M. Lee of San Francisco, for the invaluable background work on the organic, brewing, espresso, and resource sections of this book.

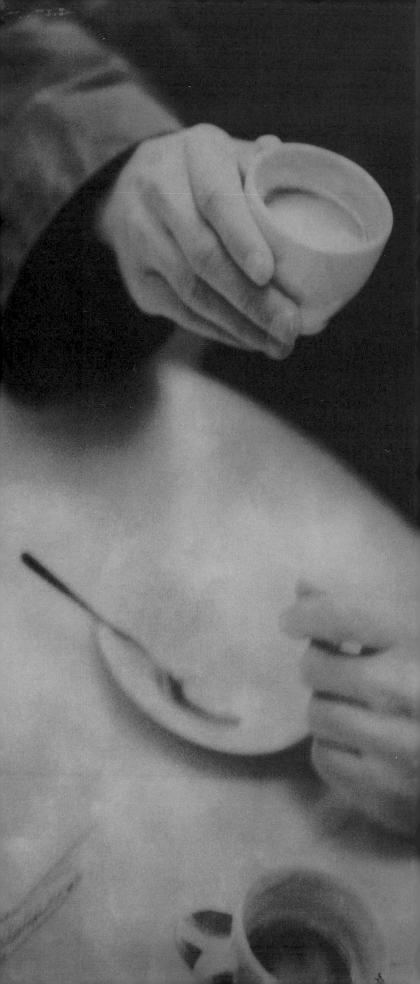

Why
A Passion for Coffee

A Personal Note

Over twenty years ago, flying to Guatemala for the first time to visit a coffee farm, I felt the elation that a struggling rock musician must feel at finally and suddenly being given the chance to play in a major stadium.* I laugh at myself now, because the act of simply visiting a coffee farm reflected no degree of accomplishment on my part. Yet there I was, saying to myself, "After all these years of struggle—drinking it in the worst dives, preparing it at home, and trying in ignorant futility (at the age of thirteen) to make a good pot of coffee with a percolator—FINALLY, I am going to see a coffee farm!"

A Guatemalan coffee plantation

Even though I visited just a few farms on that first trip, I came back with the idea that I was quite an expert. I wrote articles, taught classes, and did all I could to get everyone as excited as I was about a good cup of coffee. With each passing anniversary of that first tour, and after twenty years in the coffee business, I've come to realize how much there still is to learn about coffee, especially for me. The subject is rich and complex, and yet the end result—a good cup of coffee—is one of the simplest and most accessible pleasures available. How these two seemingly contradictory aspects of coffee can coexist is a source of continuous fascination to all who share a passion for coffee.

---

*Of your two authors, "I" in the first four chapters is written in Tim's voice.

**The Fila de Bustamante mountain range in Costa Rica,
viewed from Hacienda La Minita coffee farm**

Of course, there is a dark side to the complexity/ simplicity dynamic of coffee. It takes very little to mess up what could be a perfectly wonderful cup of coffee, turning it into absolute dreck. At every level of coffee production, choices are made: choices between expense and thrift, flavor and expedience, labor and ease, marketing and substance. Finally, the coffee drinker must make choices about what is drunk—what is chosen as the first flavor experienced in the morning or the last at night. If the tone of this book tips toward the cynical at times, it is because I believe that, too often, the wrong choices are made while all the right things are being said—even in the midst of the current "specialty coffee revolution."

Despite the many possible slips between tree and bean, bean and cup, and cup and lip, coffee has very wide appeal. What is this appeal? Nutritionally, coffee has very little to offer, except, of course, for the stimulating effects of a little caffeine; the other exception to this is a very recently discovered class of healthful antioxidants. Yet, if caffeine were the only reason people drank coffee, we would probably just pop No-Doz instead. Perhaps the antioxidant compounds exert some instinctual pull upon us, because of their potentially health-giving properties. Or possibly there are other compounds in coffee that for one reason or another appeal to our psyches for reasons that we do not yet understand—similar to the way in which dogs, pigs, and humans find black and white truffles so irresistible.

A hillside of coffee in bloom. The flowers perfume the air
with a scent like honeysuckle and lime.

The sensual perception of coffee is the reason we
drink it, then, and what we derive from it is informa-
tional as opposed to nutritional. Coffee, therefore, can be
compared to other aesthetically appreciated information
media, like musical recordings, paintings, or poems. This
may seem like a stretch, but after returning from that
first tour of coffee farms, I found inspiration and valida-
tion for this idea.

On the way back from Guatemala on that first trip, I
went to Chiapas, Mexico. I was struck by the differences
in aromas, plant life, and humidity between the farms in
Chiapas and those in Guatemala. These differences were
all the more striking because the state of Chiapas is adjacent to the Guatemalan border. When I returned from
Mexico, I brewed a cup of the coffee I brought back from

a mill in Chiapas and was immediately reminded of the air, plants, and earth of Chiapas, as clearly as if a videotape were being played for me. We have all had this kind of experience—when a waft of a particular aroma reminds us immediately and deeply of a place or person in an almost unconscious way. The aroma of coffee has literally hundreds of aromatic components and all of these had a conspiratorial effect in transporting me back to Chiapas in an instant. I hope this small (but Great) book will help to initiate such journeys for you.

The Best Coffee

This is THE question that every coffee professional is asked upon meeting someone who doesn't work with coffee: "Oh, you work with coffee? Tell me, *what is the best coffee?*"

There is a tendency with coffee, for some reason, to want to simplify it, to pigeonhole it, to explain it, drink it, and get on with it. The irony of the "best coffee" question is that it tends to lower coffee's place in the gastronomic firmament. Insisting on one best coffee suggests that coffee's realm is so limited, and its possibilities so narrow, that there could be only one truly great coffee.

The fact is *there is no one best coffee.* There are, however, a few truly superlative coffees. And there are a great many wonderful coffees. The question of which are which is one that has been known to inspire passionate debate at any gathering of those who work with coffee.

We certainly all have our favorites—and that is really the question to ask—"What are the things about coffee that you enjoy the most?" By knowing what it is you like about coffee, you can search out coffee origins, roasters, and brewing methods that deliver those characteristics. Or, if you are not so sure about the qualities you like in a cup of coffee, you might ask yourself a few more questions about what sorts of flavors, foods, and even wines you like. Based on those answers and because of the incredibly wide variety of coffees available, it might be possible to choose one that fits into your range of taste preferences.

Once you start tasting different coffees and appreciating the different flavors and range of qualities and styles of coffee available, you'll find that your taste preferences

may change radically. As you pursue further exposure to coffee, you'll find that your tastes may change yet again.

So it might be useful, or interesting, or at least diverting, to ask yourself, *before* reading this book, what your favorite coffee is. Then ask yourself again, *after* reading this book (and after, presumably, tasting a few more coffees). Finally, after a year or two, if you remember, you might ask yourself once again. If this book has been at all successful, you will name two or three favorite coffees (and each with increasing ambivalence, because

Tunisian men make coffee with traditional implements

the attributes of even more coffees you've tried or learned about will be tugging at your memory). You will know that great coffees can be sharp, fruity, and acidic, or rustically full-bodied with notes of spice and a hint of pepper. You will also know that the enjoyment of coffee would be less if there were not such extreme opposites.

THE COFFEE PLANT.

1. Section of berry showing embryo.	4. Fruit (cross section).	8. Ovary and calyx (longitudinal section)
2. Fruit (cut to show the berries).	5. Embryo.	9. Pistil.
3. Two ripened berries.	6. Ripe berries (Porto Rico).	10. Stamens.
	7. Flower (longitudinal section).	

Mysterious Origins

It is said that an Ethiopian goatherd (often called Kaldi) discovered coffee. He saw his goats cavorting in a field one day and wondered why they were acting so, well, exceptionally goaty. Noticing they were eating the fruits of a perennially struggling little tree, he tried one himself. He found the fruit of the coffee tree to be vaguely sweet and otherwise bland, yet mildly refreshing. He also noticed that after a few minutes he was feeling especially goaty himself: capering, gamboling, and cavorting around.

Realizing that the usual boundaries of propriety between a goatherd and his goats were in a state of alarming deterioration, the noble (could the discoverer of coffee be any less?) goatherd composed himself as best he could, gathered up a handful of the fruits, and took them to an abbot. The abbot tried them and thought they were a gift from God, given to him so that he and his monks could pray all night. In another version of the story, the abbot walked by the goats and the goatherd and saw what was going on, and decided he wanted the stuff for himself and his monks.

The arabica coffee tree is indigenous to Ethiopia (the home of the apocryphal Kaldi), and its cherries were first eaten there, initially as fresh fruit. Subsequently, a dried pemmican-like form was made, especially for travel, and this was either eaten straight or mixed with dried grain. These two preparations comprised, respectively, a premedieval Powerbar and a very early form of granola. (The seeds, or beans, of the fruit were not included in either.)

The usefulness of the fruit of the coffee tree thus established, the trees, or their viable seeds, were transported to Yemen and cultivated there. It was in Yemen that a sun tea made of coffee cherries, beans, and a few leaves first appeared. Shortly thereafter, in all likelihood, this sweetened sun

An Ethiopian coffee pot

tea spontaneously fermented, thereby providing the popular combination of alcohol and caffeine that today is more typically consumed in the form of Irish coffee.

This coffee wine was the first beverage to be named with the original word for coffee: *qahwah*. This word does not mean "giver of strength" as is often proposed in books and articles on coffee, but rather comes from an Arabic verb meaning "to put one off." Coffee wine "put one off" sleep when it was drunk in moderation and "put one off" essentially everything if consumed to excess. (Its recreational potential notwithstanding, qahwah was generally considered a medicinal beverage, there being other and more easily produced fermented beverages available, notably a form of mead—a wine made from honey and water.)

All of this early coffee history occurred before the prophet Muhammad established the Islamic faith. Sometime shortly after his arrival in Medina in A.D. 622 and before his death in 632, he decreed that the faithful should not consume any alcoholic beverages, purportedly

A man stands in a field of young coffee trees just transplanted from the nursery. In maturity, the trees can reach thirty feet in height, but they never lose their shrubby appearance.

due to the rampant drunkenness he found in that city. After that time only the coffee sun tea, known as *qishr*, was consumed. Qishr is still drunk today, either as a sun tea or brewed by boiling water.

It was not until the early 1400s, though, that coffee (as we know it) first appeared. This was about the same time that metal pots, in which water could be boiled over a fire, appeared in that part of the world. This made it possible for the coffee sun tea to be made more quickly by boiling leaves, cherries, and seeds in water. This combination of fire and coffee seeds probably accidentally led to the happy creation of coffee. Perhaps a pot of tea boiled dry or tipped into the fire, giving the world the first (very rustic) brewed coffee from roasted beans. Alternatively, a store of dried cherries and beans might have caught on fire and was then doused with water. In either case, coffee (as we know it) could not have been prepared without the ability to boil water.

Although a coffee tea existed for centuries, it never spread far from its birthplace. This is true despite the fact

A vintage coffee card romantically depicts the source of the beans: Brazil. These collectable cards were given away with the purchase of coffee and encouraged repeat sales.

that the tea can be made from dried cherries that could have been imported to Europe at any time before coffee (as we know it) first appeared. The attraction, then, was not the caffeine, which is contained in the tea, but the other mysterious attributes we touched on earlier.

The Spread of Coffee

Coffee spread, in starts and stops, on to the rest of the world. Much has been made in other books of coffee's controversial nature and how the debate on its healthfulness (and even, to some, its wickedness) followed it wherever it went. Suffice it to say that there are usually two groups lurking around when something new appears that is inherently yummy and consummately enjoyable: 1) those with whom nothing yummy ever agrees; and 2) those for whom the idea of someone else enjoying something yummy and convivial is just simply abhorrent. These groups, mostly the latter, have worked really hard to keep coffee from everyone's lips. Obviously, they are inveterate failures.

Controversy and all, coffee eventually made it across Europe and into England. Coffee seeds (live unroasted beans still in their husks) were transported or smuggled to all the places you might assume they were taken to: Indonesia, Central and South America, even back to other parts of Africa.

At first, coffee was drunk mostly in ways that would taste either very odd or very awful to coffee drinkers today. Most brewing instructions published during the time of coffee's introduction to Europe instructed the reader to boil the grounds for varying lengths of time and then to heavily spice and sweeten the acrid potion. The coffee of Vienna (where coffee first appeared in Europe) was at first more confection than serious drink. It took a long time for people to figure out some of the most basic things about making a decent cup of plain old black coffee—or even to determine that such a thing might actually be good. In Ethiopia and Yemen the coffee was (and still is) roasted very lightly, which heavily accentuates the coffee's fruitiness and acidity. At such a roast, the drink tastes more like mulled cider than anything most Westerners would label "coffee."

Despite the strange methods of preparation, coffee consumption continued to spread. It still does today, as coffee companies vie to introduce coffee to people and nations that have yet to wholeheartedly embrace the drink. These efforts may lead to coffee's supplanting tea as the world's second most popular drink (water being the first). How coffee will taste and how it will be roasted and brewed at that point in its history may be very different from what we know of coffee today.

A farmer displays his raw ("green") coffee beans.

The photo above demonstrates why the best coffee is selectively hand-picked: Perfectly ripe red coffee cherries (as at left) share the same branch with unripe green fruits.

Coffee Heroes

Chapters in the positive history of coffee are plentiful. Although there will always be those who try to do things cheaper (with worse results), there are others, unfortunately in smaller numbers, who always ask, "How can we make it better? What do we like about coffee? How can we make it more that way?" Everyone who drinks truly superior coffee has benefited from the work that these people have done.

A partial recounting of recent coffee heroism and milestones would certainly include the following. Although there is never a substitute for freshly roasted, one of the best packaging systems available for coffee, the one with the little valve on the front of the bag, was introduced about fifteen years ago (see page 55). Brewing equipment manufacturers, working with such groups as the Specialty Coffee Association of America, are constantly striving to produce better brewers than have ever existed. Manufacturers of roasting equipment are working with inventors of measurement equipment, such as Carl Staub of Agtron, to define what, exactly, happens when coffee is roasted—and thereby to refine the process. Swiss Water Decaffeinated is working to produce better and better tasting decaf coffees for those who can't handle caffeine. Farmers, such as Bill McAlpin in Costa Rica, who produces the exquisitely prepared La Minita Tarrazú, or the Janson family of Panama's Café Volcán Barú, are growing and processing coffee at lengths never before attempted. Eduardo Andrade of Brazil's Fazenda Vista Alegre invented a new way of growing and processing coffee that is so different, he was able to patent it and charge well over double what the average Brazilian coffee demands.

This list leaves out, of course, a most important group, the businesspeople who risk it all (or a lot of it, at least) to bring premium coffee to market. They take raw green beans from any of sixty possible countries of origin, convert the beans into a product with an unpackaged shelf life of less than two weeks, and try to sell the stuff to potential coffee lovers before it goes stale and they go broke. Roasters, large and small, work with brokers and importers and farmers to produce coffee that coffee drinkers will not only buy, but for which they will pay a premium. That premium, which *never* translates into more than pennies per cup, represents the increased value that many coffee drinkers are willing to place on the coffee they drink. It means that, while most people recognize that they will never drink the most expensive wine, or drive the most expensive car, *anyone* reading this book can drink a cup of the most expensive coffee in the world. (Pretty cool, huh?)

A Never-Ending Mystery

The most important thing to know about the history of coffee is that much of it has yet to be written. The possibilities of coffee—the range of its flavor potential, the effects of processing and roasting on flavor, the intrinsic flavor characteristics of the various subspecies of coffee trees—are all still only partially understood. Much of what is considered sacrosanct in our knowledge of coffee is actually open to question. For instance, what constitutes a good cup of coffee? Many coffee experts will say categorically, that high-grown, highly acidic, washed coffees are the best. While this type of coffee is certainly delicious, there are other, extremely popular coffees that might be described in an almost diametrically opposite fashion. What this all means is that while some opinions about coffee may be better informed than others, few that are formed in good faith are wrong. Much experimentation is still in order.

Becoming a Coffee Taster and a Coffee Expert

It may seem silly or even counterproductive to finely dissect the experience of drinking and enjoying a simple cup of joe, but the goal is really to simply maximize the enjoyment derived from that cup. Just as students of art or music find more to enjoy about their chosen fields than a lay person might, the more you learn about the taste and flavor of coffee, the more you can find to enjoy.

Advertisements for coffee over the years have talked about maximizing the *yield* from a pound of coffee. Rather than having focussed on how little can be spent on an increasingly wretched cup of weak and insipid brew, this energy might have been better spent on extracting the most enjoyment out of the best possible coffee. My hope in this book is to persuade you (if you need persuading) that the point isn't to guzzle the stuff all day long, grimacing after each excruciating sip, but to

A professional coffee taster in the cupping laboratory of the offices of the National Coffee Association of Guatemala

really savor one or two cups a day of something that is the best of its class. As I've said before, few of us drive to work in the world's best car (whatever that is), or enjoy dinner accompanied by the world's best wine, but some of the world's best coffees are available to almost all of us. What's wrong with really enjoying that cup of coffee and trying to understand what it is that you like so much about it? If your answer is "nothing," then you are on your way to becoming a coffee taster and a true expert.

To Cup or Not to Cup

The tasting procedure known as "cupping" is the coffee industry's secret handshake. It was developed by green coffee buyers as a reproducible, semiscientific method of detecting the defects in a cup of coffee. These buyers weren't anxious to find reasons for paying *more* for coffee, but for paying *less:* Cupping, therefore, puts most coffees in the most negative light possible and is not the best method for truly enjoying a cup of coffee.

Traditionally, when coffee beans are prepared for cupping, the roast is very light, so that no defects or taints of flavor will be burnt away, as might happen in a darker roast. To further tease out a coffee's foibles, cupping is done at a lower-than-ideal brew strength, so that stronger flavor components won't overwhelm a less-than-obvious deficiency. During the type of cupping that is practiced in the United States, furthermore, the brewed coffee is allowed to sit on the grounds for the entire procedure, and this certainly does not optimize taste, either. Finally, each cup of coffee is made from a few discrete beans, ensuring that a single defective bean will exert maximum impact in the small cup it occupies.

This emphasis on the negative, in the cupping procedure, is not necessarily a bad thing. But, since cupping is based on the assumption that there are always going to be a lot of defects to detect, it is not necessarily a good way to explore all the things that might be right about a cup of coffee. Many coffee professionals understand this, so they brew a pot of a coffee they are considering for purchase or sale. Once they know that there is nothing wrong with a particular lot of coffee, they can find out what is right about it by tasting it as the final consumer

How to Cup Like a Pro

Ritualistic in form, cupping sessions involve several steps. Coffee professionals perform visual examinations of the green coffee, and then they roast, smell, and taste each sample. Each step reveals clues about a coffee's quality and character (or in many cases the lack thereof).

To set up your own cupping session you'll need $5^1/_2$- to 7-ounce glasses (two or three glasses for each different coffee being cupped—highball glasses work best), a scale, a grinder, and a kettle. Home coffee roasters, which are available in specialty retail stores and on increasing numbers of web sites, enable anyone to set up a fully functional cupping session.

If you are not roasting your own beans, buy the lightest roasts you can find for your first few cuppings. If you choose to roast your own, roast them as lightly as possible. If you want to compare coffees from different origins, then it is important to find ones that are roasted to the same degree. Even then, keep in mind that two roasts of identical color can have completely different flavor and taste profiles, depending on who roasted them.

If you are starting with unroasted coffee, take some of it before you roast it, and hold it in your hands. Stick your nose in it and breathe out, warming the coffee, and then very gently breathe in (don't breathe in the beans!), paying attention to the aromas you'll notice. You won't detect familiar coffee smells, but you may notice something later in the cupping that is reminiscent of what you smell now.

Start by setting up two or three glasses for each coffee you want to cup. Weigh out 7 grams of roasted coffee beans for each individual glass, and grind them to a medium to medium-coarse consistency; put the ground beans in the glasses. Grind the beans separately for each glass, so you will be able to see if a coffee is "even," or consistent, from cup to cup. Many well-sorted, washed coffees, such as Costa Rican La Minita Tarrazú and La Torcaza Estate, are absolutely even from cup to cup. Other coffees, especially dry-processed coffees such as those from Yemen, are less even and you may notice that each cup you set up is different. This is not necessarily a bad thing, since most people make coffee by the pot and not the cup, but it is interesting to note, and it can explain why certain coffees do not always taste the same.

Now, smell the freshly ground coffee by holding your nose to the glass and cupping your hand over the glass and your nose to form a seal that prevents aroma from escaping. Make note of the aromatic characteristics you perceive.

Next, bring cold water to a rolling boil. Do not allow the water to boil vigorously for a prolonged period, since this robs the water of oxygen and makes the coffee taste flat. Pour the boiling water over the ground coffee, but note that even the manner in which the water is poured is important. Instead of pouring the water all the way to the top of the glass, it works better to fill the glass halfway, making sure that the water is evenly distributed over the grounds (a slight shaking of the wrist when pouring water from the kettle helps).

Let the coffee cool for a few minutes, and then "break the crust" by scooping up a spoonful of the wet grounds, which will have floated to the top of the water. Keep your nose very close to the top of the glass as you do this. Inhale deeply, trying to detect the aromatic characteristics of that particular coffee. Once this step is complete, finish pouring the water to the rim of the glass. Wait a few more minutes for the coffee to cool and for most of the grounds to sink to the bottom of the cup. When the cups are ready to taste, clear all the grounds and foam off the top by skimming the surface of the coffee with a soupspoon. If it takes more than one or two skimmings to clear, the coffee probably has not yet cooled enough.

If you are trying to teach recalcitrant children proper table manners, do not let them watch you cup coffee, because the next steps are to slurp, chew, and spit. Using a round spoon, slurp the coffee into your mouth, being careful to spray your entire mouth. The coffee should splash on all parts of the tongue simultaneously, since different areas of the tongue are responsible for different taste perceptions. "Chew" the coffee, or swish it in a back-to-forward motion inside your mouth. This allows you to discern the body. Finally, you may want to spit the coffee out so that you do not become too full or too caffeinated, and because swallowing does not enhance one's ability to discern flavors. (Although it is hoped that all the coffees you taste will be so good you won't be able to resist!)

of the coffee will—brewed for enjoyment, not the vivisection of cupping.

This is not to say that you should not "try this at home." Certainly it's fun to do, once. And while cupping does allow you to compare several different coffees in a simple and straightforward manner, it will only give you the illusion of coming to understand what a particular coffee is all about, or what it can yield in terms of flavor and enjoyment. Keep this in mind, because many people mistakenly believe that if they can't instantly appraise a coffee by briefly slurping it up and spitting it out, they will never come to understand coffee or appreciate its nuances. Appreciating a cup of coffee is a very different experience than cupping it, and this is something that takes time, even for a seasoned professional.

After grasping the basics of the cupping procedure, the next step is far more difficult: recording and communicating all the sensory data that the coffee yields. The approach is at once scientific, technical, and sensual: scientific, in that the procedures should be reproducible (that is, repeatable both in terms of the procedure and the results obtained); technical, in that each aroma, taste, and flavor, and every nuance in mouthfeel, should be as accurately described as possible; and sensual, because the evaluation relies on one of your most primitive senses, the sense of smell.

What Are You Looking For?

The experience of coffee actually comes to us through several different senses. The most important of these is the sense of smell, which allows us to perceive the aromas of coffee. When you experience these aromas while actually drinking coffee, they are experienced as flavors. These perceptions are different from those that come to you solely through the sense of taste—sweet, sour, salty, and bitter. It is important to distinguish from what you may experience through the chemical contact on your tongue and in your mouth of certain substances, like salt, and the infinitely more varied perceptions you perceive as flavors, through your sense of smell. To highlight this difference I refer to experiencing tastes, for the sense of *taste,* and savoring flavors, for the sense of *smell.* This may not be the only correct or accepted usage in the

Green coffee, processed and ready for roasting

coffee trade (or any other field for that matter), but it's a simple and straightforward way to deal with the discussion at hand.

After the senses of smell and taste, the next most important sense in experiencing coffee is that of touch. You actually touch the coffee with your lips, tongue, and palate when you sip it, and you form a tactual perception of it, including whether its consistency feels thick or thin, watery or syrupy (a coffee's "body"), and also whether it is astringent (a puckery sensation having nothing to do with sourness or acidity). The temperature of what you are tasting is also important, influencing what you smell and taste, and prejudicing you about what you taste. The texture of a coffee is also an important aspect of your experience of it; some coffees, no matter what sort of filter is used, seem grittier than others. Wet-processed coffees tend to have a smoother texture than dry-processed coffees. Dry-processed coffees can be perceived as gritty, but some of the best have lots of body and are grit-free—as smooth as washed coffees.

Finally, some attention should be paid to how a coffee "finishes," as they say in the wine trade—what it tastes like in your mouth after you have swallowed it. Savoring the aftertaste of a coffee is something that can stay with you for several minutes (or up to half an hour in the case of espresso). After the last sip is swallowed, a

A Selection of Descriptive Terms

A Selection of Descriptive Terms

This glossary has been adapted from terms found in the *Coffee Cupper's Handbook* by Ted Lingle, published by the Specialty Coffee Association of America. In many cases, a very idiosyncratic spin has been put on a particular definition by this author, as in the cases of "savor" and "taste," for instance.

Acidity A tart, tangy, lemon-like taste experienced on the tip and side of the tongue; a flavor element much prized when found in specialty coffees. (Also called **Brightness.**)

Aged A coffee that has been stored in its country of origin, usually in a dried but unmilled state, and generally for a period of three or more years; the coffee loses moisture, gaining body and a distinctive woody or earthy characteristic in the cup.

Aroma The sensation or smell of gases released from brewed coffee. This can include a perception of astringency or acidity via the vapors. (Compare to **Fragrance**.)

Aftertaste All the sensations of a coffee experienced after swallowing it (or spitting it out).

Astringency Not a taste or flavor but the physical sensation of "puckeriness."

Balance When all of the perceivable components of a coffee work together harmoniously on the palate. No one flavor, taste, or perception dominates the experience.

Body The viscosity or "thickness" of a coffee; part of a coffee's overall mouthfeel. Common adjectives used to describe body include light, medium, full, thin, watery, syrupy, heavy, rich, and creamy.

Bouquet This usually means the total aromatic profile, including aroma, fragrance, and aftertaste. The world of coffee, however, needs a term to describe the aromatic sensations arising from the roast rather than from the nature of the coffee itself. In the wine trade, "bottle bouquet" refers to the aromatics arising from the bottling and aging of a wine as opposed to those that are intrinsic to the grapes. "Roast bouquet" might be a useful term to describe the aromatic components contributed by the roasting process.

Break To break into the top layer of foam and grounds that have not settled to the bottom of the glass during cupping. (See also **Crust.**)

Brightness See **Acidity**.

Complexity The presence of many flavors and tastes complementing body, astringency, and long aftertaste. Inextricably linked to balance, because if any one component dominates another, then complexity will not be detectable.

Creamy A texture that is reminiscent of cream. (See also **Body**.)

Crust The top layer of foam and grounds that have not settled to the bottom of a cupping glass.

Earthy A flavor characteristic reminiscent of soil. Often used in a positive manner to describe the taste of Sumatran or Sulawesi coffee; used as a pejorative to describe other coffees.

Flat Lacking a noticeable fragrance, aroma, and aftertaste.

Flavor The perception of a coffee's aromatic compounds (those detected by the sense of smell) when the coffee is in your mouth.

Floral An aroma, fragrance, or flavor characteristic reminiscent of flowers; usually found in the coffees of Kenya and Ethiopia.

Fragrance The smell of a particular ground coffee. (Compare to **Aroma**.)

Grassy An aroma, fragrance, or flavor characteristic reminiscent of freshly mown grass; considered an unpleasant attribute.

Herbaceous An aromatic experience of various herbs, but often specifically referring to grassiness. Often accompanied by bitter and astringent components as well.

Mouthfeel All of the tactual perceptions a coffee has to offer throughout the process of drinking or cupping it.

Musty An aroma, fragrance, or flavor/taste characteristic reminiscent of a burlap sack; often occurs as a result of poor storage, insufficient drying, and/or aging.

New Crop An aroma, fragrance, or flavor/taste characteristic of freshly harvested, freshly milled coffee, which tends to be acidic and especially floral.

Nutty An aroma and/or flavor characteristic reminiscent of nuts.

Palate Used in this book to decribe all the sensory equipment used to experience coffee; NOT used to describe a part of the mouth.

Past Crop An aroma, fragrance, or flavor/taste characteristic reminiscent of burlap, straw, wood, or grass; occurs when green coffee is old and loses a significant amount of its moisture and acidity.

Piquant A term used to describe the acidity of coffees that are characterized by a sweet, tingling sensation experienced at the tip of the tongue when one first sips the coffee; prevalent in good coffee from Kenya.

Sample Any offering of green or roasted coffee being cupped.

Savor To specifically experience aromatics when a coffee is in the mouth (when the aromatics are therefore flavors).

Spicy Having to do with aromatics reminiscent of various spices, detectable either when smelling or tasting a coffee.

Taste The perception of specific chemical compounds on the tongue and in the mouth via the taste buds. Possible perceptions are sweet, sour, salty, and bitter. The word "tasting," however, often refers to the entire range of sensory perceptions, incuding flavor, body, and so forth.

Texture This refers to a coffee's relative "smoothness" or "grittiness" when it is drunk or sipped. Distinct from body and astringency, though usually heavy-bodied coffees and dry-processed coffees will tend to be grittier than washed, light-bodied coffees.

Winey A flavor characteristic reminiscent of red wine; typical of coffee from Kenya or Yemen.

good coffee will have even more flavor, taste, and tactility to reveal, and all of it should be pleasing.

A Question of Balance

Of all the attributes a coffee can have, perhaps one of the most crucial is that of "balance." You can have some of the world's best musicians playing together in a room, but if they aren't playing in harmony, the listening experience is not likely to be very pleasing. Some coffees are incredibly fruity, but if they are totally lacking in body and acidity they are unlikely to be the ones you will choose to brew in the morning. Many people, when they first begin to explore coffees and taste different blends, gravitate toward obvious flavors and characteristics. There is nothing wrong with this, but you may find that over time you will enjoy a Sumatran coffee, for example, that not only has heavy body, but a hint of acidity and fruit as well—one that sacrifices a little body for a smidgen of brightness and clarity. The difference is subtle, and only the best roasters and retailers will sell coffees that offer this extra level of sophistication, but at some point you may want to try to find them.

Finding the Right Words

In communicating the experiences derived through the five senses, words are the currency of all that you perceive. The more primitive the sense, the more critical language becomes in expressing its perceptions. If you and a friend look at a painting, you can say that it is beautiful or evocative and your companion can be more or less expected to understand. If there is any doubt, you can refer to some particular aspect of the painting—you can even point to that aspect—and there can be no doubt as to what you mean.

When it comes to taste and smell, however, pointing to something is much more difficult. The intimate perceptions that sail, glide, and sometimes, unfortunately, trample across your palate are much more personal; you can never be sure that your dining or drinking companion experiences what you do in the same way.

There is also an illusory sense that what you see is somehow more substantial than what you smell, although, in reality, this is not the case. In fact, when you smell something, you are actually directly detecting molecules of the thing you're smelling, which in this case have floated up and away from the steaming coffee and into your nostrils. When you see something, you are only sensing the light waves reflected from the object that you're looking at. So, although sight actually provides an indirect method of perception, it carries with it much greater authority. "Seeing is believing," after all.

When you are describing smells and tastes you encounter in a particular coffee, your words must be as descriptive as you dare make them. The words you use will never be absolutely precise, but you should recognize their importance and make every effort to use them to their full descriptive capacity. The more you do so, the more enjoyable and memorable your tasting experience will be. Further, with the right words at your disposal, you will be able to better share what you perceive with others.

Describing what you experience in a cup of coffee is important for two reasons. Perhaps most obviously, it serves to communicate what you perceive to others. You can say, for example, "Yuck, this is cruddy coffee!" or, "Wow, this is amazing coffee!" You can also be much more precise, citing specific reasons why you like or dislike a coffee, pointing out to someone else something to appreciate about a particular coffee, or identifying a defect.

A more important reason for finding the right words to describe a coffee is to be able to create reference points within your own mind, so you can compare the coffee you're drinking now with other coffees you've tasted before. Without these reference points your experience will be much more vague. While you could still say, "Gee, I like coffee A better than coffee B," you would not be able to say, "Gee, I like coffee A because it is not quite so fruity, but it still has a nice note of dried cherries, and the same syrupy mouthfeel as coffee B." Becoming able to describe such preferences is no big deal, it just involves getting comfortable with associating words with the tastes, flavors, aromas, and tactual perceptions you experience.

In the coffee business there are many words that are used to describe defects. But, if you are buying coffee from a conscientious roaster, your problem should not be identifying what has gone wrong with a coffee, but rather what has gone right. In this regard, much work has been done recently to develop a vocabulary of useful words, but most of these have yet to be universally accepted. In this book, we have included a brief glossary of words (see pages 22–23) that you might use to describe a coffee's favorable attributes as well as some common defects. These words should make more immediate sense as you thoughtfully taste a few coffees—particularly if you taste them side by side.

In describing a particular coffee, it is important to pay as much attention as possible. It may sound ridiculous, but take notes. Notes not only preserve your experience, but the act of taking them also forces you to verbalize, in a way that makes sense and is specific, exactly what you experience.

Go slowly. Smell the dry grounds, smell the grounds during the brewing process, and smell the freshly brewed coffee before taking a sip. Then, don't be afraid to slurp, thereby aspirating as many of the aromas and flavors of the coffee as possible. Think of specific, unique words that capture the essence of what you are savoring and tasting. Don't be content to pluck words from a glossary of accepted terms. Rather, reach into your own experience for the most precise and meaningful description you can find. Sometimes the description that is the most precise for you will be based on a very personal experience that you had of another aroma or flavor. Maybe you burnt pecans once as a child when endeavoring to make cookies, and a certain coffee might recall that aroma. Oddly enough, it is often these most personal recollections that will clue someone else in to what you are tasting.

Coffee tasting spoons

There is no "wrong" terminology or description. For example, Kenyan coffees are often described as fruity, winelike, or even as having a black currant note to them. Occasionally, lesser Kenyan coffees are noted for their tomato-like character in the cup. The variation in coffees, especially those from Kenya, is greater than these few terms reveal, however. Try to find the term that most accurately describes the particular coffee you are tasting. If something seems fruity at first, mentally run through all the fruits that you can think of until your mind lands on one that rings a bell. You won't always find the right word, but you will find that with practice the search becomes easier.

In developing an informed coffee palate, the important thing is not to be afraid of seeming silly for taking a simple cup of coffee so seriously. The taste and flavor of coffee, after all, is why you drink the stuff. Extracting more experience from every cup is the only way to really make your coffee yield more.

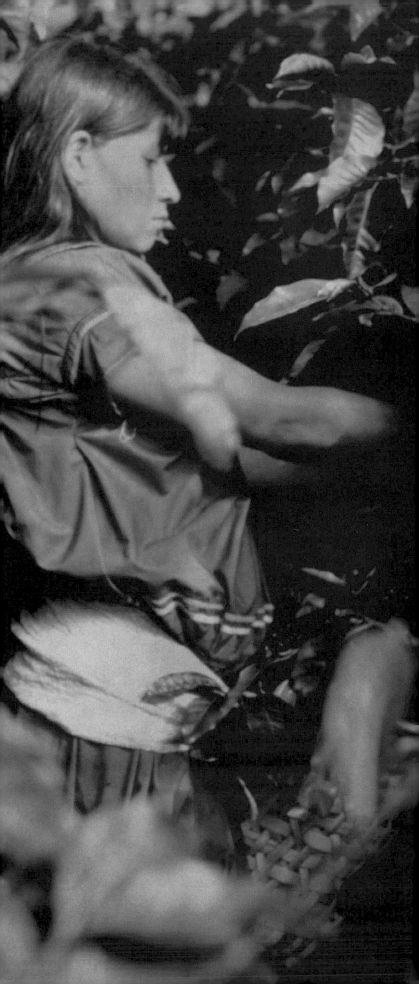

Where

The Origins and Production of Coffee

The Coffee Tree

The coffee tree has medium to large leaves and tends to be spindly and mangy, particularly when it is devoting its energy to producing fruit. Although it can grow to thirty feet in height, it never quite shakes a certain shrubbiness. This primitive, hardy plant exhibits a feast-or-famine mentality that it learned in the mountains of Ethiopia, where *Coffea arabica* is indigenous. The coffee tree will shut off all but the most essential functions in the face of a draught or other stress. During a good year of mild temperatures and generous rainfall, however, it will thrive and produce abundant amounts of fruit, grabbing at the chance to procreate but nonetheless exhausting itself for the next season or two. This inconsistency is one of the reasons why the price of coffee is so changeable.

There are many species of coffee trees but only one that produces coffee you'd want to drink—*Coffea arabica*. Another species, *Coffea canephora* (known informally as "robusta" due to the unsettlingly robust vitality with which it flourishes) produces a beverage that is undrinkable and only vaguely reminiscent of real (arabica) coffee. (In fact, everything about the robusta tree is creepy, from its prolific rate of growth to its resistance to many diseases that could stop an arabica tree dead in its—admittedly limited—tracks, to the very evil way it tastes.) Robusta coffee is so cheap, however, that many roasters cannot resist using it—primarily because there are many uninformed coffee drinkers who do not care what passes their lips.

Unripe coffee cherries already show varying rates of growth.

THE SHADE-GROWN DEBATE

The first commercially planted coffee crops did not do well in full sunlight. So, coffee farmers planted various types of taller trees in amongst their coffee trees, providing at least partial shade. This is "shade-grown" coffee. (Newer, more disease-resistant and higher-yielding coffee hybrids grow better in full sun, eliminating the need to plant shade trees.) Now, professional and amateur bird lovers are telling coffee lovers that by insisting on shade-grown coffee they can support "bird-friendly" farming practices that provide a habitat for many different species, including migratory songbirds that spend their summers in North America. (Coffee trees themselves are too low to the ground, too densely covered with leaves, and too close to human contact to provide suitable nesting sites for most birds.) Many coffee experts also believe that the older, shade-grown hybrids produce higher-quality, better-tasting coffee. But the case of shade-grown hybrids is not a simple one. In many microclimates it's possible to grow older varieties without shade trees. Other farmers have land that doesn't attract migratory birds at all. Some farmers with newer varieties set aside nesting areas for birds (really, they do). It is also unfair to assume that any coffee farm not in strict accordance with shade-growng guidelines is fundamentally unfriendly to birds. Some recent research has found no correlation between declining songbird populations and coffee farming practices in Central America. (On the other hand, a worldwide domesticated cat population growth has resulted in a documented, measurable decline in the numbers of songbirds.) All in all, while the idea of buying "shade-grown" coffee is well-intentioned, it is not necessarily one that should be followed blindly.

(On this level, however, it must be stated that most roasters recognize that the cheapest, raunchiest, most defect-ridden arabica beans can taste even worse.) Some robusta apologists argue for its use in blends, even in specialty coffees, particularly espresso. The other species in commercial use, chiefly *Coffea excelsa* and *Coffea liberica*, produce coffee so vile that merely looking at these beans, with their pointy ends and conchlike shape, will give you a major case of the heebie-jeebies. Their taste is consistent with the appearance of the beans.

There are several different subspecies or varietals of *Coffea arabica* that are worth noting. Each subspecies of the coffee tree will produce a different tasting coffee,

depending on where it is grown. It is often said that the best-tasting coffees are produced from the older hybrids of coffee trees, particularly *Coffea arabica typica* and *Coffea arabica bourbon*. These are not always the best trees to plant, nor do they always produce the best-tasting coffee in a given locale. Which tree a farmer chiefly employs depends on many factors, including elevation, average rainfall and temperature, presence of diseases and pests (which may afflict some trees more than others), soil, and the farmer's predisposition and/or ability to use fertilizers and pesticides—as well as the type of coffee desired. No single variety of tree has proven itself to be superior in all cases to any other. Each tree and the beans it produces seem to respond differently to the unique combination of soil, temperature, and rainfall that each farm provides.

Origins and a Sense of Place

Where a coffee comes from has a big impact on its taste. "Where" can mean a lot of things: the global region, country, local area, and individual farm all influence the final product. To begin with, arabica beans, like wine grapes, grow and develop their character best under certain topographical and climatic conditions. "High-grown" arabica—coffee that is grown in mountainous areas in equatorial countries—is synonymous with the highest quality and the most complex character.

The great coffee-growing regions of the world lie in a belt around the equator. The coffees produced in each of these regions usually have sets of general characteristics associated with them. Within the regions, individual countries, such as Guatemala or Kenya, and areas within those countries, such as the city of Harrar in Ethiopia or the state of Chiapas in Mexico, are also understood to produce coffees with certain qualities. At the finest level, individual farms or even parts of farms can present us with highly distinctive coffees—much as individual vineyards can give rise to unique wines.

The wine analogy is a helpful one. Coffees, like grapes and the wines they produce, are subject to countless variables that affect their quality. Their character—everything from the health of the particular tree to that year's rainfall,

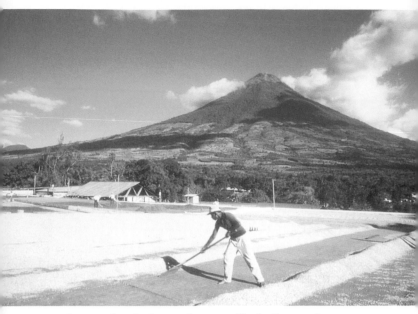

A man rakes drying parchment coffee in Guatemala.

from local agricultural traditions to the individual expert-
ise and efforts of growers, producers, and roasters, has its
effect. So while it is convenient to talk about the origins of
various coffees—and important to know about them in
general—it's just a starting point in learning to judge and
enjoy superior coffee. Coffee is always changing, and it's
not that easily pinned down. This complexity may make it
difficult for anyone to authoritatively name "the best coffee," but it sure makes exploration and experimentation
worthwhile.

The Great Coffee-Producing Regions

More than the national origin of a particular coffee, it is
useful to know what region of the world it is from and
with what traditions of agriculture and processing it was
produced. There are basically five great regional categories of arabica coffee produced throughout the world.
The first region is defined by the mountains of eastern
Africa; the second by the mountains of the Central American isthmus; the third is, well, Brazil; and the fourth
encompasses the island coffees between the Indian and
Pacific Oceans. The fifth "region" is a catchall category for
island coffees, including Hawaii and Jamaica.

Q & A

Q. *What is Mocha/Java coffee, and does it have chocolate in it? Why is it spelled so many different ways?*

A. Blending deep-bodied, smooth, old Javas with bright, fruity, complex, and wild Yemeni coffee is often considered the best, if not the original, coffee blend. Mocha, the chief port city in Yemen, came to mean the coffee shipped from it. Because Yemeni coffee can be so fruity and complex, it was often thought to contain chocolate, and hence the association between the Mocha name and a chocolate/coffee combination.

The trouble today is that the best coffees from Java and Yemen are very rare and have a concomitantly high price. (A great Javanese coffee, in fact, has become an oxymoron, so mediocre are Javanese coffees today.) This has inspired any number of ruses and schemes to convince the consumer that Mocha/Java isn't a blend of particular coffees at all, but rather a "flavor style." Misspelling "Mocha" has come to be a subtle disclaimer, implying that maybe the coffee in the bag isn't from Yemen at all, in fact. In short, it is spelled so many different ways to confuse you. Coffee marketers know that the romance and exotic allure of the "Mocha/Java" name is an irresistible siren call for the coffee consumer, and they will do anything they can to benefit from this attraction and still remain one step ahead of labeling laws.

One alternative blend deserves mention. Ethiopian Harrar coffees are reminiscent, in their wild complexity and fruity notes, of Yemeni coffee. Harrars, though, are darker, fuller bodied, and not as "chocolatey," even though when they are very good they can be nearly as expensive. Java/Harrar, a more accurate term, is actually an excellent blend, and it deserves to be labeled properly. But, then, you might be even better off with a good (and less expensive) Sumatran coffee, which is probably closer in taste to what a great Javanese coffee used to taste like. So, next time try Sumatra/Harrar. It might live up to the hype of Mocha/Java, at far less cost!

Eastern Africa and Yemen

The first great region includes the birthplace of coffee, Ethiopia. The mountains that begin in Yemen, on the Arabian peninsula, are broken by the Red Sea and continue down through Kenya, Tanzania, Zambia, Malawi, and Zimbabwe, and even South Africa. These countries produce coffees that tend to be fruity, acidic, and medium-bodied, with hints of various berries, dried fruits, and raisins—depending, as always, on the exact area where each coffee is produced and the method of processing.

The coffees of Ethiopia are both wet- and dry-processed (see pages 47–49 for an explanation of these terms). The dry-processed coffees, from Djimmah, Ghimbi, and Harrar, to name a few regions, are traditionally full-bodied, with an almost roasted spice and cooked fruit flavor. The washed coffees, from Limmu, Sidamo, and Yirga Ch'efe (known as Yrgacheffe on many coffee menu boards) have floral notes that, at their best, are delicate yet intoxicatingly fragrant. (Other, more average examples of Yirga Ch'efe's coffee exhibit a cooked lemon note and, while thoroughly pleasant, are no substitutes for the much-prized, rarer version.)

Processed coffee beans ready for export

The coffees of Yemen, all dry-processed, are known for their wildly fruity flavors, which result from the longer time the cherries spend between being picked and being thoroughly dried. Working in favor of the Yemeni farmers is the coolness and the high altitude of their land, as well as the diverse, multivarietal nature of their plantings. Coffee, once it is picked in Yemen, does not begin to ferment immediately as it might in a lower, warmer, and more humid environment. In the best examples, the coffee develops a gentle fruitiness that is almost sweet and cherrylike. The flavor is also complex and ever changing.

Nations adjacent to the row of countries just described also produce excellent arabica coffees but have traditionally had trouble getting wide acclaim for them. Ongoing political troubles in the region have not helped. For years, a few European firms have quietly bought most of these coffees and used their high ratio of flavor-to-cost to benefit their blends. These coffees can have an exceptionally wide range of sweet and fermented fruit flavors along with a heavier body like that of lower-grown coffees. In the blends that they traditionally occupy, they contribute interesting flavors without dominating.

The Central American Isthmus

From the northernmost origin of Mexico southward along Central America toward Colombia and Peru, the coffees of this region tend toward neutral and medium-bodied yet acidic. From microclimate to microclimate, however, there are distinct differences. Coffees from Oaxaca tend to be the most characteristically Mexican, with a slight hint of nuttiness (perhaps hazelnut), backed by medium body and clean, clear notes of acidity. The state of Veracruz is also a significant coffee producer. But the heart of Mexican coffee production is in Chiapas, Mexico's southernmost state. With their full body, strong acidity, and aggressive flavor, these coffees could almost be mistaken for Guatemalan coffee from the department of Huehuetenango, to which Chiapas is adjacent.

Coffees from Guatemala are becoming more widely known for their regional differences. Antigua, the most famous of Guatemala's coffee-producing areas, produces elegant, almost smoky coffees, with strong acidity and delicate, nuanced flavors. There is a lingering fruitiness in coffees from Antigua that is reminiscent of cognac. Coffees from Fraijanes, south-east of Antigua, are sharper in their acidity and more straightforward; they are well known for being solid blenders, but not for drinking on their own. Coffees from the area around Lake Atitlán are also acidic, but with greater body. Cobán, one of the least-known areas of Guatemala, produces some of the country's least-understood coffees. Coffees from

Carl Janson of La Torcaza Estate in Panama cups coffee from a pending harvest.

Cobán are not known for their acidity, but for their unusual flavors: a pleasant woodiness that is almost cedarlike, a slight spiciness, and a characteristically bitter finish. Alternatively, they can be extraordinarily fruity in a sweet, direct, and clean manner, which offers the roaster the ability to make a blend with the fruitiness of a Yemeni coffee without having either to pay for one or to work with the forbidding complexity that a Yemeni coffee might contribute.

Coffees from El Salvador and Honduras are not often seen sold as single-origin coffees. They are good, but few are considered great. Honduran coffees are mostly fuller bodied and lower in acidity. Salvadoran coffees can be excellent in acidity and elegance but have tended to lack complexity, although farmers there are working hard to change this. Pacomara, a varietal new to the market and now produced in El Salvador, may help.

Coffees from Costa Rica are known for being some of the most "coffee-like" coffees of all. What they lack in unusual flavors, they make up for in full-speed-ahead coffee flavor, balance, power, and acidity. The best are clean, clear, and powerfully acidic, with deep flavor and medium to heavy body. Some Costa Rican farmers (those from Tarrazú and the Dota Co-op near that region) also produce coffees that are slightly, almost mysteriously, fruity. La Minita Tarrazú is one of the cleanest and most powerfully flavored coffees in the world, used as a standard by roasters to compare against other washed coffees—even among those who don't actually buy it.

Panama is lost between two giants of coffee production, producing only a tenth of the amount of coffee grown in Costa Rica, its northern neighbor, and an even smaller fraction of the amount grown in its neighboring Colombia, to the south. Its coffees tend to be gentler, milder versions of Colombians and Costa Ricans. Most of the coffee is produced around Volcán Barú. To the southeast of this mountain, the famous coffees of Boquete are produced. Grown in what is primarily a high-altitude cloud forest, the coffees tend to be slightly fruity, the Lerida farm producing one of the best examples. To the northwest, the Barú region produces coffees that are more straightforward but perhaps less complex. At their best, they exhibit a slight butterscotch note. La Torcaza

Q & A

Q. *A coffee retailer has a list of "varietal" coffees from Guatemala, Costa Rica, and so forth. What does he mean by that?*

A. Many people in the coffee business are confused about varietals. In the wine business, the word "varietal" means the subspecies of grape with which the wine is made (for instance, Chardonnay is a varietal). In the coffee business, people have started calling single-origin coffees, like Guatemalan coffee, "varietal" coffees—and this is wrong. Like grapes, coffee has varietals—*typica, caturra,* and *catuai* are just a few of the fascinating subspecies whose merits and deficiencies the coffee-obsessed ponder into the wee hours of many a night. These are botanical categories, and have nothing to do with countries of origin.

Estate is on this side of the mountain. Finally, on the northern shoulder of the Barú volcano, the region known as Paso Ancho produces the well-known La Florentina estate coffee and El Tucán (a trademarked coffee from a particular, undisclosed farm).

Colombia can produce over ten million seventy-kilo bags of coffee a year, which, as noted earlier, vary widely in variety and quality. Perhaps victims of their country's own marketing, the farmers of Colombia seem ambivalent about selling all their coffee as if it were a single type—despite the regional differences of the coffees and the varying dedication and competency of the farmers. To describe the various regions of Colombian coffee production and the coffees' characteristics would be impossible here. But, because Colombia comprises such a large coffee-producing area of similar soil and climate, there are some unifying themes in the flavors of the coffees it produces. These include above-average body, good acidity, and a characteristically caramelly note. Some coffees grown at very high elevation, from older hybrids, rank as some of the world's best. Other areas, where new disease-resistant (and flavor-challenged) hybrids are heavily planted, produce coffee often noted for harsh and bitter overtones.

Venezuela produces coffees very similar to those produced across its Colombian border. At their best, Venezuelan coffees are somewhat lighter bodied than

Coffee pickers in India wait to have their coffee weighed so they can be paid.

Colombians and can be very acidic. Since Venezuelans drink most of the coffee that their country produces, the coffee is seldom seen elsewhere.

The farmers of Peru also produce coffee, but the quality is acceptable only to high-volume roasters. Peru is a big producer of average-quality organic coffee. The volume of coffee from Bolivia is slight and the quality is generally undistinguished. In both countries there are a few quality-conscious farmers trying to produce better coffees, but the mediocre reputation of both origins makes this an uphill battle.

Brazil

The other great coffee region of the Western Hemisphere is Brazil, defining, with its full-bodied, naturally processed coffees, one of the few truly national styles of coffee, distinctively and immediately recognizable. The Brazil flavor, full, forward, and a tad grainy, is well known to consumers, even if they do not know that the light-roasted coffee they drink in donut shops and fast-food outlets usually has a good percentage of Brazilian coffee in the blend. There is a new effort and momentum in Brazil to gain recognition for its coffees in the specialty markets, and many farms, including Fazenda Vista Alegre, are working hard to change the reputation of Brazil's coffee from that of a "useful blender" to that of an extraordinary specialty coffee.

The Islands between the Indian and Pacific Oceans

The island coffees grown between the Indian and Pacific Oceans are in some ways a disparate group, but they have some distinctive characteristics as well. They include coffees from Java, Sumatra, Timor, and Sulawesi. These coffees are uniformly of thunderous body and range in texture from downright gravelly to a smoothness and fullness bordering on that of heavy cream. Acidity is generally low, and flavor nuances tend toward spiciness, as opposed to the fruitiness of the East African coffees.

Perhaps the biggest exceptions to the preceding description are the coffees of New Guinea. Acidic and clean, they are in many ways more reminiscent of Central American coffee. Yet they still have a telltale syrupy consistency signalling their kinship with Javan and Sumatran coffees. While not really a member of this group, up-and-coming India should be mentioned as a producer of uniquely heavy-bodied coffees, with a characteristic spiciness and distinctive texture. It is tempting to find parallels between India's coffees and those of Brazil, as both produce similarly full-bodied coffees so dense they are almost gritty, with the better ones having hints of spice, tobacco, and roasted nuts.

Other Island Coffees

"Other island" is a catch-all category of exotic coffees, which often sound more romantic than they taste. These include those of Hawaii in general and, in particular, those of the Kona Coast, as well as those of Jamaica, Puerto Rico, and even the Galapagos Islands. These coffees tend to be mild, neutral, and at their best, very clean with a hint of acidity. The very best can be exceptionally well balanced, with a slight hint of

An Indian woman with coffee cherries

warm spices, including cinnamon and allspice. While sometimes very good, these coffees are seldom, if ever, worth the high price they generally command—thanks to their exotic reputations and strong base of tourist fans (who buy the coffee while travelling and then seek to recapture the experience at home).

What's in a Name? Single-Origin Coffees

Where a coffee comes from does have a big impact on its taste. But saying that a particular origin—for example, Colombia—produces coffee of one particular taste is unfair to the coffee, the farmer who grew it, and the country where it was produced. (It is more convenient for marketers, particularly those with a big job like marketing *all* of the coffee from Colombia, to classify the coffee from one country as having the same flavor.) In fact, Colombia even has several distinct growing regions that produce coffee during different times of the year (due to the country's position straddling the equator). The coffees produced in these regions are often more different from one another than from coffees grown in Venezuela or Costa Rica. Mexico, Guatemala, Costa Rica, and Panama also have discrete regions producing distinctive coffees. Indonesia is perhaps the best example. Two of its most well-known coffees, those of Sumatra and Java, are never referred to as Indonesian, but rather as Sumatran or Javan.

Another complicating factor in the discussion of origin character is the impact that the coffee roaster exerts. Some highly regarded roasters do not identify the single-origin coffees beyond the country they came from. While the sign on the bin may simply say "Guatemalan," it is really shorthand for "What we think a really great Guatemalan coffee should taste like." Not only does the roaster roast that coffee to the point they like, but if they're really good at what they do, they will carefully select their Guatemalan coffee to match the style they are looking for, year in and year out. Achieving consistency from one year to the next for a given origin is not easy. Variations in weather cause changes in the taste of coffee grown during a particular season. These changes in character may be greater in one part of the country than in another.

Estate Coffees

To make matters more complicated, coffees may even differ within a single farm. Some farmers know that certain areas of their farm produce different or better coffees than other areas. This may be due to great variations in elevation from one part of the farm to another, but it can also be because of variations in microclimate from one side of a mountain or valley to another. The farmer himself also has a great impact on the taste of the coffee produced. The trees chosen, the methods of agriculture and processing, and the level of effort expended on these tasks all will have an impact on the taste of the coffee. Often, this will differentiate the coffee from other beans produced in the same region to such a degree that the coffee is either considered separately or the region's reputation changes based on the taste of the coffee from that particular farm.

The farm, in fact, is the single most important thing to know about a coffee's region. In some cases, a close-knit group of farmers comprise what is essentially a single farm. These farmers work together, either officially as a legally established cooperative or more informally, to produce uniformly excellent coffees. This is possible only if all the farmers included have the necessary trees, farming practices, and elevation. Additionally, central processing at one mill is necessary for the coffee produced to rise to the level of quality and consistency obtainable from a fine estate. (The Dota Co-op in Costa Rica is an example of such an arrangement.)

Coffee cherry blossoms

Women sorting coffee cherries

Much has been made of estate coffees, and justifiably so. These coffees are prized because they often have a distinctive and unusual character and are frequently considered the ultimate in specialty coffee. It is worth getting to know a particular estate coffee over several years. This way, you can appreciate the difference in crop years as well as the consistent personality that the estate coffee will always display. At the most basic level, it is the farmer who grows the coffee and who decides what that coffee will be. Coffee grown by an excellent farmer in a mediocre region will taste better than coffee from a carelessly run farm in an excellent region. (The following sections, which explain the crucial steps of coffee cultivation and processing, demonstrate why this is so.)

The trend in coffee production today is toward higher volume in general, with a few dedicated diehards focussing on producing the best coffee they possibly can. Increasingly, finding exquisite coffees among the range of qualities available will become a difficult task. The roaster is the coffee drinker's last line of defense against mediocrity and the primary link between the coffee flower that first gives rise to the bean, and that steaming, perfect cup of coffee. Finding a dedicated and discriminating roaster should be far more important to you, the coffee drinker, than finding the best farm or the ideal coffee-producing region. How can you tell? You'll taste the difference.

Two Beans and a Cherry

Coffee beans grow inside the fruit of the coffee tree—a green "cherry" ripening to bright red, with a thick skin and very little pulp. Depending on the variety of tree, it will take three to seven years for a coffee tree to produce fruit. Inside each cherry, two beans are usually found, with their flat sides facing each other. If only one bean develops, it does not develop a flat side but grows into a small, egg-shaped bean known as a "peaberry."

The coffee cherry arises from a blossom that appears briefly, sometimes for less than a day, six to ten months before the cherry is fully ripe. In certain parts of the world, particularly near the equator, it is not unusual to see ripe and unripe cherries along with new blossoms all on the same tree. Such areas, notably Colombia and Kenya, produce a small crop of lesser quality six months after the main crop.

Cherry Picking

When the cherries of the coffee tree are ripe, it is critical that they be picked and processed promptly. Ripeness, and the degree of care taken to pick only the ripest cherries, are some of the most crucial aspects of coffee cultivation and processing, since they relate directly to the quality of the coffee that will be produced. This means that the coffee pickers must pick each cherry carefully by hand and that each tree must be picked over several times in one season, as the cherries ripen. Farmers who want to encourage their workers to pick only the ripest cherries must pay them considerably more for the cherries they pick: Obviously, the more selective the pickers are, the fewer they will be able to pick per day.

Farmers producing lower-quality coffees, on the other hand, discourage their pickers from being selective, by paying very little for the cherries picked and accepting cherries of all manner of ripeness, including green, undeveloped cherries. Pickers on such farms usually just grasp the branch near the center of the tree and pull everything, leaves and cherries, off at once. The coffee from farms using this method of "strip" picking tends to be rough and harsh.

Top: **At La Torcaza Estate in Panama, the volume of coffee cherries is measured to pay pickers.** Inset: **On the same farm, a picker selectively hand-picks the ripest cherries.**

Mechanical picking, while it would seem to be the least selective method, can actually be more selective than strip picking. A large metal arch on big rubber tires is driven next to a row of coffee trees. On each side of the arch, long vibrating rubber rods on a rotating column pass through the branches of the coffee trees and shake off the cherries that are at least somewhat ripe. The green cherries, clinging more strongly to the branch, stay on until the next drive-by of the mechanical coffee harvester. By irrigating carefully to ensure more uniform blossoming and ripening, a farmer can further maximize the utility of his harvesting machine. But he'll still never produce truly great coffee, and most farmers set the harvester to maximum vibration, achieving the same degree of selectivity found with strip picking. Great coffee is not their concern.

The Wet and the Dry

Aside from the cherry skin and pulp, the coffee bean has two other layers that must be cast aside before the bean can be roasted: a sticky, slimy mucilage coating and a thin husk known as "parchment" or "pergamino." Developing the most economical yet quality-conscious methods of removing these four layers from the bean has been the coffee farmer's challenge for the past six hundred years.

A Dry Husk

The first coffee farmers decided that the easiest way to remove the fruit and husk from the bean was to let the whole thing dry and then to grind off everything at once. This method of processing, called the "dry" or "natural" process, has remained essentially the same since it was first developed in Yemen and Ethiopia hundreds of years ago. Its use spread to other areas where coffee was grown, including the Dutch East Indies, India, and Ceylon. Coffee processed this way tends to have fuller body and grittier texture, less brightness or acidity, and flavors of earth and warm spice. Notable examples are Ethiopian Harrars, Yemeni and Sumatran coffees, and most Brazilian coffees. Contrary to what many people suppose, dry processing is not always the cheapest method. In Brazil, for example, it is much cheaper to process coffee using the wet method because it is faster—and, in a country with a traditionally high cost of capital, this makes all the difference.

A VOLATILE COMMODITY

Coffee is famous for its boom or bust cycle, as any consumer who watches grocery store prices will attest. The problem is that the volatility of coffee as a commodity has discouraged farmers from consistently trying to grow the best coffee they can. All their efforts at producing and marketing a truly superb coffee can be trivialized by one random event of weather, war, trade embargo, or currency devaluation—making it more profitable to simply wait for the next disaster to cause the market to skyrocket. In the meantime, many farmers feel they are better off spending as little effort or money as possible on their coffee, in case the market plummets.

A Wetter Way

It was not until coffee was brought to the Western Hemisphere that it became absolutely necessary to find another way to process it. Farmers in the West Indies found that coffee trees grew well on their land, but the coffee tended to rot in the cherry, not drying, due to their more humid weather and frequent rains. In order to prevent the fruit from fermenting before it dried, spoiling the bean inside, the fruit was quickly removed with whatever means were available. Often, this was done by slaves who smashed the fruit with their feet and then rinsed the beans from the fruit with fresh water.

Next, the beans, still in their parchment husks, were spread on the ground and dried in the sun. Then the dry and brittle husk was removed—at first with rock or wood grinders. This method, called the "wet" process, was first developed more than two hundred years ago. It produces "washed" coffee with an entirely new taste profile. Cleaner, lighter, with more brightness and almost no earthiness, washed coffees have come to be viewed by many as superior to naturally processed coffees. Central America, Colombia, and East Africa still offer the best examples of washed coffees.

Today, the key to producing the better washed coffees is the additional sorting or selection of beans that occurs as part of the process. In moving the beans from pulper to fermentation tank and from tank to drying patio (or drying machine), the beans are conveyed through washing

ABOVE AND RIGHT: Wet parchment coffee being channelled from fermentation tank to drying patio

channels that tend to move lighter beans faster than denser beans, which are thought to be better. This way, processors can separate their coffees into "firsts," "seconds," and, sometimes, even "thirds."

Wet but Less Wild

By the end of the nineteenth century, the wet process had become well established, and each of its steps had become more refined. Machines had been developed to "pulp" the coffee, that is, to remove the fresh cherry skin and pulp from the mucilage-covered parchment husk and the bean inside. Another step—fermentation—had been added, which removed the mucilage covering by allowing the pulped coffee to sit in tanks for up to a day covered in water. Naturally-present microbes broke down the slimy mucilage. At the same time, this step seemed to add greater acidity to the coffee.

Since then, some processors have begun to skip fermentation and remove the mucilage with high volumes of fast-moving water. This "aquapulping," they say, preserves more sweetness in a coffee—but it may tend to mute acidity. Because it is faster, it is cheaper, and therefore increasingly favored by many processors. Whether it is better tasting or not will be up to the marketplace to decide. Still other processors are now leaving the mucilage on the parchment through the drying step, which yields an even sweeter, fuller-bodied coffee, but with even less acidity and brightness.

Dried, Milled, Delivered—It's Yours

The parchment-covered coffee can be dried on concrete patios, on wood-framed screens sometimes called "kenyas" (because of their use in that country), and in large drum-shaped

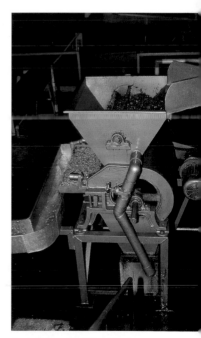

A pulping machine removes the skin and pulp of the cherry from the coffee bean.

dryers. While much is claimed for sun-drying the parchment coffee—that it is more acidic, more flavorful, and so on—the best drying method should be determined by the prevailing conditions at a particular processing facility. Often, the best coffee is produced using a combination of drying methods.

In the ongoing automation of coffee processing, mechanical milling, or removal of the parchment husk, has seen further refinement and evolution. Additionally, mechanical sorters of various types have been developed to classify raw or "green" coffee according to size, density and, with the advent of light-sensitive electronics, even color and reflectivity. Many processors, though, still swear by a final step of hand sorting, even after the best light sorters are used.

Once the coffee has been dried and sorted, it is ready to be bagged and exported. It is important to note that not all coffee growers are coffee processors. Many small farmers in Colombia and Central America sell their coffee cherries to middlemen, who then sell the truckloads they collect to processing facilities called *beneficios*. Still other farmers have "wet mills" where they can take the coffee down to the dried parchment stage. These farmers then sell their coffee to a "dry mill" (a beneficio), where the processing is completed.

A truck outside an Ethiopian processing mill

Dry milling is as critical, and as controversial in its impact, as any other stage in coffee growing and production. The first step of dry milling is the removal of either the dry parchment or the entire dry cherry husk (depending on how the coffee has been processed up to this point). This removal is usually done in machines that press the husks and beans through metal rollers; these rollers are spaced so as to remove husk from bean without mangling the bean too much. The degree of care taken with this step can be important. Speeding too much coffee through this step can overheat the beans and crush a few in the process, making for an uneven roast and further diminishing the quality of the final product.

Grading—Pass or Fail

Unroasted coffee beans, now free of cherry, parchment, mucilage, and all but 11 percent of their moisture, are ready to be sorted and bagged for export. Sorting the beans according to size, density, and freedom from defects will have an important impact on flavor. While consumers tend to pay a premium for the biggest beans, it is often the case that the midsized beans are the brightest and best tasting. Colombian Supremos, for instance, are the biggest grade of Colombian beans sold, and the most expensive. However, the smaller Colombian Excelsos, all else being equal, are far more flavorful.

Each country has its own standards for grading the various export qualities of coffee it ships. Grading is usually done based on a combination of factors that include the elevation at which the coffee is produced, the size of beans, and the freedom from defects in the taste of the coffee. The higher a coffee is grown, the harder the beans are thought to be, so the degree of hardness is also an ancillary factor (higher-grown Guatemalan and Costa Rican coffees, for example, are graded "Hard Bean" and "Strictly Hard Bean"). Many countries, including Costa Rica and Guatemala, have national coffee offices, responsible for tasting each lot of coffee produced for export and approving it before it is shipped. In theory, at least, tasters evaluate whether a coffee is good enough to be shipped and whether it meets the grade as it is described on the invoice.

Grading coffee beans in Ethiopia

Generally, the best coffee comes from operations where all steps in processing are controlled by the farmer who grew the coffee. The farmer has the most at stake in maximizing the value of his crop. Processors who don't grow coffee, and who have no control and perhaps no specific knowledge of the quality of the coffee they are processing, may not take as much care unless they are processing a coffee that will be shipped under one of their own brand names.

If one thing is important to remember when it comes to processing coffee, it is that the whole subject is a relatively new one. Wet processing is a little over a century old, and coffee (as we know it) is only five centuries older than that. During the past few centuries, remarkably little has been done to determine what effects various cultivation and processing methods have on the production of coffee.

Decaffeinated Coffee

There is perhaps no area of coffee lore more filled with misconceptions and outright misinformation than that of decaffeinated coffee. Perhaps it is because decaf coffee has to live or die strictly on its taste, unlike regular coffee, which, at its worst, will at least provide some stimulation. This dilemma leads coffee purists to some unfair assumptions about decaf coffee drinkers: that they don't care about the taste of their coffee, or that they are not really coffee drinkers at all but wimps who don't have the guts to drink a real cup of coffee. The truth, recently discovered by one of the decaf processors mentioned here, Swiss Water Decaffeinated, is that most decaf drinkers also drink regular coffee. They say that taste is the most important factor in selecting their decaffeinated coffee. In fact, most decaf drinkers drink regular coffee until they can't take any more caffeine; then they switch to decaf because they still crave the flavor of coffee— hardly coffee wimps!

The Basics of Decaffeination

While there are countless patents for various methods of decaffeination, there are basically only three that are commonly used on a commercial basis: nonwater solvents, such as methylene chloride; supercritical, highly pressurized carbon dioxide; and water processes such as the proprietary Swiss Water. All involve dissolving the caffeine out of green coffee beans, and each has its relative merits and shortfalls in terms of cost and quality. It is generally considered safe to drink decaffeinated coffee produced by any of these means.

The one step common to all methods of decaffeination is the initial process of presoaking or steaming the green coffee, allowing the beans to swell to about twice their size. As the beans swell, their surface area increases and their cellular structure opens. The beans are then introduced to the solvent of choice, and the caffeine inside each bean slowly migrates into the solvent. In each method, the beans are then rinsed several times with fresh solvent to ensure that as much caffeine as possible is removed. In most processes, close to 98 percent of the caffeine normally found in a particular coffee is removed.

THE VALVE BAG

These packages of coffee with the funny-looking "belly button," or "valve bags," as they are generically known in the industry, actually represent a great leap forward in coffee packaging. As coffee roasts, many chemical changes occur. Flavors develop and some compounds break down while others are formed—starches, for example, generate simple sugars, which then caramelize, giving roasted coffee its brown color. One of the by-products of these reactions is the formation of carbon dioxide gas, which builds up in the cellular structure of the coffee beans and is released slowly over several hours after roasting. But once coffee is roasted, it is vulnerable to staling from exposure to oxygen in the air. The challenge, then, is to keep oxygen away from the coffee, thereby losing as few aromatics as possible, and still allow the beans to release the excess pressure of the gas from the roasting.

The valve bag overcomes these problems by packaging the coffee in an oxygen-free environment immediately after roasting. When the beans in the bag begin to de-gas, excess pressure escapes through a small valve embedded in the packaging material. This valve only allows gas (and as few aromatic compounds as possible) to go out of the bag—no oxygen seeps in. Squeeze the bag and you will hear air escape from this valve. You will also be able to smell the coffee, and it should smell fresh. While the valve bag is certainly not a replacement for freshly roasted coffee, it has allowed coffee drinkers access to reasonably fresh coffee on a far wider basis, and in greater variety, than was possible twenty years ago.

The Taste of Decaf

So what should a good decaf taste like? It should taste like a great cup of coffee. True enough, any kind of processing will alter the flavor of a coffee, but the key is to keep this alteration to a minimum and to preserve as much of a coffee's original character as possible. Most good roasters who care about the quality of their regular coffees also take a lot of trouble to ensure that their decafs are equally tasty. A few, however, give their decaf line less attention than it deserves, so it pays to shop around for the best decaf you can find. You should be able to tell all this in one sip—and that sip is far more important than knowing which solvent is used.

When buying decaf, it is important not to assume you are getting a particular type of decaf. Many roasters, for example, will mislabel the chemical decaf they sell as

Organic Coffee —
Fact and Fiction

Organic Coffee —
Fact and Fiction

Organic coffee is coffee grown without the use of chemical pesticides, herbicides, or fertilizers. Certified organic coffee has been
verified as having been grown using organic methods and practices, by an independent certifying agency. Unfortunately, there
is a range of thoroughness in certification—from a ritual visit of
two to three hours, once a year, to the well-enforced require-
ments of an ongoing commitment to an agricultural system. The
issue is sufficiently complex that roasters who seek to offer coffees that are truly organic send their own buyers or representa-
tives to the farms or co-ops in order to ensure that they are getting what their customers are paying for.

The clear, indisputable benefits that might be ascribed to organic coffee cultivation are related more to the environment and the
health of coffee farmers than to the health of the consumer or the
quality of the product. No evidence to date has been found to
suggest that organic coffee is actually healthier for the coffee
drinker than nonorganic coffee. Even organic movement advo-
cates de-emphasize the purported health threats from chemical
pesticides used in commercial coffee cultivation. Unlike many
other organic agricultural products, such as tomatoes or carrots
found in local supermarkets, coffee goes through thorough processing before it is consumed. The skin and fruit of the cherry is
removed, the seed is fermented and washed, and then the seed is
roasted at temperatures that generally exceed 400°F; in addition,
the brew we drink is actually 97 percent water. Thanks to all these
factors, it is usually the case that even coffees grown with the
use of several different chemicals will pass sensitive laboratory
tests with flying colors.

By focussing solely on the organic certification seals, consumers
may not be getting the best-quality coffee. Some certified-
organic estates without ideal soil or sufficient elevation may
have sought certification less out of a commitment to quality
than as a means of capitalizing on the organic movement and
some consumers' voracious appetite for anything labeled organic. Higher-grown specialty coffees often do not require the pesticides and herbicides that are needed for coffees grown at lower
elevations. Many fine coffees are pretty close to organic by

default. The farmers growing these coffees, however, are often reluctant to commit themselves to an organic-only means of production because they know that unforeseen infestations, weather changes, and other such problems might necessitate the use of some sort of chemical treatment.

Many coffee roasters, brokers, and buyers, particularly in the specialty segment of the coffee industry, insist that quality should be the foremost concern for consumers, and that by remaining quality-focussed, a consumer is likely to support many of the same environmental goals sought by the organic movement. Quality-focussed growers have a natural tendency to adopt some organic farming practices simply because their goals are similar: healthy trees, fertile soil rich in potassium, nitrogen, and phosphorus, and processing methods that yield clean coffee. Many of the methods practiced by organic farmers have long been in use by well-run traditional farms. The skin and pulp of the cherry, for example, have traditionally been used as compost; dry parchment husks are used as an efficient source of fuel to supply the heat for mechanical dryers. Additionally, organic agriculture is not always sustainable. Farmers using organic methods may actually have less chance of staying in business or maintaining livelihoods for their workers. In this complicated matter, as in many other aspects of the coffee trade, the simplest test may be the most effective: Does it taste good? If it does, it has probably been grown in a sustainable way and, for the most part, in balance with nature.

"European Water-Processed," believing their customers will be more comfortable buying a water-processed, chemical-free decaf. There are also different water processes available and retailers often do not indicate which one was used in the coffee they are selling. It is important, therefore, to ask your coffee retailer specifically what type of decaf they sell, right down to the plant or company that processes it, since there are often wide variations in quality from processor to processor. A few quality-conscious retailers choose their own coffees for decaffeination and send them to the decaffeinator who they believe will do the best job. These "toll-processed" coffees usually taste far better than the less expensive coffees that many decaffeinators offer "off-the-rack." If your retailer describes such a toll-process procurement procedure, you are likely to be buying some of the best and freshest decaf obtainable. (Toll-processing is often preferable because otherwise many decaffeinators will use the least expensive type of a particular coffee, believing that their customers only care about price: They're often right.)

Finally, it is important to know that the decaffeination industry is in a state of flux and that many retailers may not be up to date. Swiss Water, for example, recently completed a re-engineering of their entire process, and this significantly improved the quality of their decaffeinated coffees. Certain large retailers, however, have not yet had the opportunity to inform all their staff members of this change. Additionally, many other decaffeinators are either improving or completely retooling their processes. As with all things relating to coffee, the only way to find the best decaf is by tasting and comparing.

Roasting: A Fiery Art

From blossom to cup, the history of a coffee is a series of trade-offs, approximations, and compromises. Picking the coffee at a certain level of ripeness accentuates certain characteristics while minimizing others. Processing coffee in one particular way favors one group of attributes in the cup and diminishes others. As a coffee gets closer to the lips of the drinker, the trade-offs become more critical, the path more treacherous, and the poten-

The cooling tray of a small shop roaster

tial for disaster far more imminent. During brewing, the potential for making a bad cup of coffee can reach house-of-horrors proportions (but more about that in the next two chapters!).

During roasting, the intervening craft of the roaster offsets these dangers. Flavors can develop, die, or never emerge in the roasting process, which culminates in a phase where the beans are essentially on fire, burning from the inside out. It is during these last few moments of the roast, under the watchful eye of the coffee roaster, that the beans will develop their full potential.

The Roasting Process

There are two basic types of roasting systems, the drum and the fluid bed. The drum roaster turns the beans inside it while they are heated by some combination of hot air and hot metal. The balance of these two, the degree of heat applied, airflow, and, some say, humidity are the essential factors in this roasting system. Fluid bed roasters create a "fluid" bed of very hot, fast-moving air on which the beans tumble about until they achieve

Raw coffee beans being sorted for density. Much of the quality of a roast depends upon the green beans that are chosen.

the desired degree of roast. There are also some hybrid systems based on a combination of very fast moving air and mechanically induced movement of the beans.

Many changes occur as raw green coffee beans are roasted and their internal temperature is lifted from room temperature to somewhere between 400° and 450°F (just short of outright ignition). As the beans increase in temperature, the water in them turns into steam and expands, their cellular structure begins to rupture, and they begin to crackle audibly: This stage is known as the "first crack." Just as the first crack finishes, the beans begin to rapidly change in color from dry green to a more vibrant green as the moisture is forced out, and then to a straw color, then caramel, and then to a darker and darker brown. The color changes signal the breakdown of starches into simple sugars and their recombination through the process of caramelization. It is during these browning stages that the stage called "second crack" begins. The browned bean is initially flat and dull in color, but it quickly becomes flecked with oil. If the beans are removed from the roaster at this stage, the oils will be reabsorbed as the coffee cools. If the roast is allowed to progress much longer, these oils will remain as a coating on the outside of the bean.

The beans also expand by almost 100 percent as they approach the end of the roast. The darker the roast, the greater their expansion. During this process they become brittle, which allows them to be ground so their flavor can be extracted.

The Flavor Debate

Beyond color and size, however, the flavor of a coffee changes the most radically during the roasting process. Light-roasted coffees tend to exhibit a great deal of acidity and fruitiness and have, in general, flavors more reminiscent of the coffee fruit and blossom itself. The darker a coffee is roasted, the more it acquires the flavors we associate with fire, smoke, and oil. The aroma changes from one of wine and roses (if you will), to that of cigars and even beef. (In fact, there are compounds in dark-roasted coffee that are identical to those found in grilled meat.) Finally, as a coffee approaches the darkest regions of the roast spectrum, it takes on the flavors of burnt wood (in a sense, all that's left of the beans at that point).

This is not to say that a coffee roasted to a certain degree of darkness will yield a particular flavor. It is possible to roast two batches of the same coffee beans to exactly the same color, and yet roast them in such different ways that it is difficult to imagine (or taste) they were once the same beans. Despite this, roasts are usually described by their degree of darkness and not their flavor—all the way from a light, cinnamon roast to the darkest French or Italian roast.

Much controversy exists as to how roasts should be named, and basically, no two roasters use identical names for their roasts. This problem has become more complex, since some roasters have even begun to trademark new names to describe their particular style of roast. This is actually not such a bad thing, because it dispels the notion that there is any universal language with which to describe roast style and degree of roast, and it serves as a reminder of the importance of roast style on the taste of coffee.

Remember, though, that for trademarked roasts, another variable is the type of raw coffee each roaster chooses to roast. The choices that a roaster makes here can obviously vary in quality, but they can also demonstrate the roaster's aesthetic preference. This decision is seemingly invisible, since most roasters don't identify their coffees beyond country of origin or proprietary blends. The styles of roast are the biggest differences

The alchemy of roasting takes the beans from their rubbery raw state to aromatic, brown, and ready for grinding and brewing.

between two Colombian coffees, for example, from two different roasters. But the differences between those styles begin with the choices that each roaster makes, as to the green coffee they procure and the equipment in which they roast it.

All roasters agree that green beans themselves would make lousy coffee—the tough, rubbery little things would ruin any grinder, and the coffee they might make would be closer in appearance to pea soup than coffee. On the rest of the roast continuum, however, there is no such unanimity. One perfectly valid philosophy argues that the best coffees should be roasted light to preserve all of their nuances and flavor, and that lesser coffees can

be more fittingly roasted dark, where delicacy won't be missed alongside the heartier flavors of the dark roast. Another school of thought holds that only with the world's finest, highest-grown coffees, from the best origins, and processed with the washed method, is it possible to combine the caramelly assertiveness of a dark roast with the brightness, zesty acidity, and intriguing fruitiness found in a light roast. As you can see, it all gets pretty complicated.

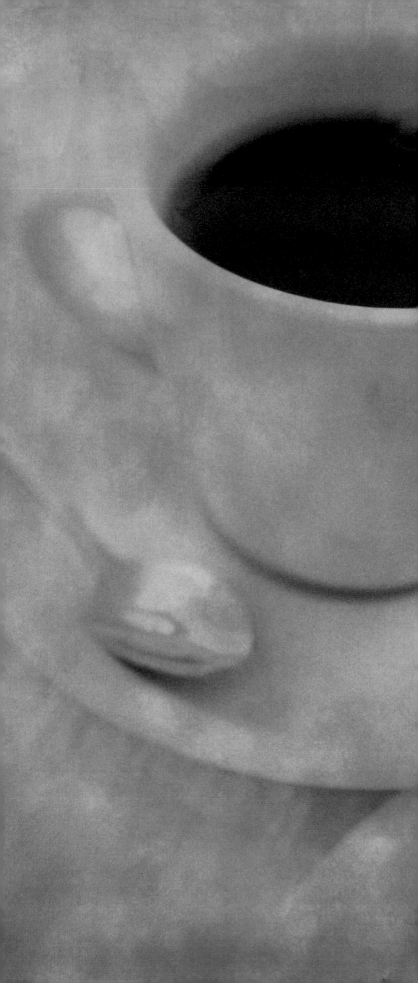

How

Brewing Perfect Coffee

Buying Beans

In your search for great coffee beans, don't get stuck on the large retail coffee chains. Start local: Try the coffeehouse around the corner. A busy shop is a good indicator that the coffee is turning over fast enough that the beans you buy will be fresh. Once you have found a good local shop, you can use it as your home base and then venture out to try other coffees. Mail-order companies and the grocery store are two good points of departure.

There are also many excellent, devoted "microroasters," as they are now called, who may have the more exotic (and rare) coffees that larger roasters are unable to offer. Often, small roasters can also focus on quality, unpressured by shareholders, and are more likely to offer a higher level of service than large chains (who may be more worried about opening stores than selling you the right pound of coffee). This is not to say that larger roasters, both those that operate retail stores and those that sell to other shops, don't have their strengths as well. Since they've grown larger and more experienced, they can frequently offer a more consistent product. They might also have greater access to some rare coffees, because they have the resources to establish contacts in origin countries.

An assumption that may limit your search for the ideal bean is that after tasting and disliking one version of a particular coffee, a Guatemalan, for example, you conclude that you don't like any coffees from that origin. However, remember that Guatemala has several distinct regions of coffee production, each producing coffees that are so different from one another that they might as well be from separate countries. It is worth trying another Guatemalan coffee from another roaster, then, to see if their version might be more to your liking. Odds are it will be roasted differently, and it may also be from another region of the country. This "second opinion" principle holds true even for estate coffees. You may find that the roast alone becomes a big factor in your appreciation of a particular coffee.

Many roasters do an excellent job of providing well-roasted, fresh coffees. By taking the opportunity to explore and taste the wares of several different practitioners, you will be able to get a better and better idea of where your

Bins of various coffees at a microroaster

preferences lie. You may find that over time, you begin to settle on one particular coffee—many people do. But it is almost always worth it to try the occasional coffee from a new roaster or origin. You will always learn something every time you try a new coffee, even if you don't like it. Who knows? You might even find the fabled "best" coffee!

High-Fidelity Brewing

I like to think of coffee as a form of information storage. Locked inside a coffee bean is a record of the weather, the land, the tree, and the labor that produced it. For that information—the flavor and aroma of that coffee—to be intelligible, much less enjoyable, it has to be brewed correctly.

Brewing is to coffee what a stereo system is to recorded music. You can have some wonderful tunes, but without the right equipment your music will sound terrible. That great coffee you just bought will disappoint you if it is not brewed properly. Brewing extracts as many of the desirable flavor elements as possible and puts them in an aqueous solution we can drink and enjoy. Again, the music analogy comes into play: We cannot hear music, or anything else, without air to carry the vibrations to our ears, and we cannot taste coffee without water to carry the flavors and tastes to our palates.

SIMPLE RULES
FOR
MAKING ∗ COFFEE,

Use ONE part Coffee to EIGHT parts water—*i.e.*, To one cup even full of dry ground Coffee, use eight cups of water.

Have your Coffee ground as fine as ordinary granulated Sugar, or so that the larger particles will not exceed in size the head of a pin.

Place your Coffee in the pot, and pour the boiling water on it. Be sure the water is boiling. Then allow the entire contents to boil three minutes (not longer.)

Then pour into the hot Coffee a large tablespoonful of Cold Water; this will force the grounds to the bottom and render the liquid clear as wine.

Serve as soon as these directions are completed. A delay of fifteen minutes will allow much of the aroma and flavor to escape.

CAUTION.

BE SURE your Coffee Pot is thoroughly cleansed, in Hot Water, immediately after each service. A cup of good Coffee cannot be obtained from a pot in which the Coffee grounds have been allowed to remain.

Always measure your Coffee and Water. Do not guess at either, but follow the exact proportions each time.

Be sure you use Boiling Water.

The above rules apply to the making of COFFEE in the plain, old-fashioned cylinder Coffee Pot. Should you use a Patent Pot, follow the directions accompanying it.. Respectfully yours,

CHASE & SANBORN, Boston, Mass.

OUR FAMOUS COFFEES FOR SALE BY

Brewing should not harm the flavor components as it extracts them, and it should extract as few undesirable flavor components as possible. To optimize extraction, brewing should occur over a period of four to six minutes and the water should be between 195° and 205°F. The ratio of coffee to water should be the equivalent of four ounces of coffee to sixty-four fluid ounces of water. While this may sound simple, it is something that few home brewing systems will do consistently. Even brewing with a filter cone and a pot of boiling water, many people will under- or overextract their coffee, or brew coffee that is too strong or too weak. When brewing is finished, roughly 10 percent of the water used will have been absorbed in to the grounds and approximately 20 percent of the coffee, by weight, will have been extracted into the brew. A really bad cup of coffee can be both overextracted and too weak, if the coffee is ground too fine and too little is used. Or, it can even be underextracted and too strong, which might be achieved by grinding too coarse and then using too much coffee. Besides a brewing method that works well, brewing the best coffee requires two other essential components—freshly roasted and ground coffee, and good water.

Freshness

The freshness of coffee, although not strictly part of the brewing equation, is nonetheless essential to making a good cup of coffee. If coffee is not fresh, it will not matter if it is roasted to perfection from the best green coffee and brewed expertly: It will taste awful. If a bakery served or sold stale bread, most people would probably notice and complain. Likewise, everyone knows that if you don't store bread properly and eat it promptly it won't stay fresh for more than a few days. Nor can you expect much of a life span from produce or meat. Yet, somehow, people expect their coffee to last and last and last.

Coffee, once roasted and kept in a cool, dry place in whole-bean form, will stay fresh for a week or so before it will noticeably start to deteriorate. First, it will lose the aromatic power that it initially had a day or two out of the roaster. Then, after about two weeks, it will start to stale, tasting more and more like wet cardboard with each pot brewed. How fast a coffee turns stale depends on the type of coffee it is; how it is handled, stored, and packaged after roasting; and how you handle it after you buy it.

Coffee should be stored in an airtight, clean glass or glazed ceramic container. Unlike plastic or metal, glass and glazed ceramic do not absorb flavors and can be thoroughly cleaned in between each use. If you purchased your coffee in a valve bag, transfer it to a storage container only after you have opened it for its first use. If you are not going to use all of your coffee within two weeks or so, you should probably freeze the portion not used. Once you start using the frozen portion, use only the beans that you need for the pot or cup you are making, and put the rest back in the freezer. When ready to brew, thaw the beans for about half an hour before grinding.

This advice is worthless, of course, if you don't buy your coffee fresh. When you open the bag you've just purchased, the beans should smell luscious and vibrant, even before being ground. If they don't, they should at least not smell like rancid corn oil and wet paper. The valve bags that have become so popular only work if they are used properly by the roaster packaging the beans, and they often are not. So don't assume that coffee will be fresh just because you buy it in a valve bag. If it doesn't smell right when you open it, try another brand, or go to a specialty coffee retailer that sells coffee fresh out of the roaster.

Grinding

The fineness of the grind and the fineness of the filter should be paired so that the grinds stay in the filter basket and the flavor goes into the coffee. The coffee should not be ground so fine that it either goes into the coffee (as a fine grind might with a metal mesh filter) or clogs the filter and extends the brewing time (as fine grinds will do with a paper filter). Conversely, coffee should not be ground so coarsely that it is underextracted. The fineness of grind also has an impact on brewing time as well as extraction. Brewing methods that work quickly, such as espresso, need a finer grind. Other methods, like the French press, can be timed for the maximum six minutes, and therefore work best with a very coarse grind. If you have any doubts about the grind you need, read the man-

Storage bins feed beans into grinders for espresso coffee.

ual for the brewer you own, or ask at a good specialty coffee shop what fineness of grind you should use .

Once you know the fineness of grind you want to use, getting it may prove a bit more difficult. The inexpensive rotary blade grinders will not produce an even grind, and so grinding coffee for a French press or for espresso is extremely difficult. The blades inevitably pulverize a small amount of coffee into a powder suitable for making Turkish coffee, while leaving other grounds too large, or even leaving whole beans almost untouched. When using one of these grinders, it helps to grasp the body and top of the grinder with both hands and shake it sharply while continuing to grind. This serves to circulate the beans and grounds in the grinding chamber, creating a somewhat more even grind. If you do this, you can get a grind that is even enough to use with a French press if you are careful not to overgrind. (If you have difficulty pushing down the plunger in a French press, the coffee is too finely or too unevenly ground.)

Burr grinders have two rough discs set a measured distance from each other. This distance is adjustable, allowing for many different grinds for many different brewing methods. The coffee beans are usually broken up into coarse chunks by a turning screw and then fed between the discs, one of which is turning. While no method is perfect, burr grinders produce a much more even grind, which leads to brewed coffee that is much more evenly extracted. In addition, most brewing methods will probably work better with coffee ground using these grinders. Unfortunately, a good burr grinder will cost at least three times what an inexpensive rotary grinder costs, with the best ones running into hundreds of dollars.

Espresso machines are more finicky with regard to the grind of the coffee: A minuscule adjustment can have a dramatic effect on the taste and appearance of the brewed espresso. When making espresso, grind is so important that you are actually better off having your coffee ground for you when you buy it (and only buying what you will use in a day or two) than using a rotary grinder. Alternatively, you can invest in a good grinder for espresso. But, unfortunately, that does mean *invest*—they can cost upwards of $200. Furthermore, grinders for espresso are precision machines expressly made for espresso preparation; they won't double as grinders for other brewing methods. For more tips on getting a good espresso grind, see pages 89–91.

There is one strength in the otherwise weak resume of the rotary blade grinder, and that is its usefulness in grinding for Turkish coffee. Here, the rotary grinder excels and can achieve a powder as fine as the best burr grinders—just grind until you no longer hear any coffee grounds getting knocked around and you will probably have a powder as fine as you could wish. (You may need to pluck out a few broken beans that have nested in the powder and thereby escaped pulverization.) The important thing to know is that however you grind (and even an electric blender will do in a pinch for all methods except espresso), you should always grind your coffee immediately before brewing. This will produce the best flavor.

Water

The point is often made that since brewed coffee is more than 97 percent water (depending on the strength of the coffee), the water you use to make your coffee is extremely important. While this is certainly true, it should not send you on an endless quest for perfect water for brewing your coffee. Water that you find good enough to drink by itself will probably make fine coffee.

In many cases, tap water is actually as good as, or better than, filtered, purified, or bottled water. This is because the water you use to brew your coffee should have a certain minimum mineral content. The problem is that many tap waters contain components that noticeably intrude on the flavor of coffee. Often, a simple charcoal filter is the best solution for this problem. If you live on one of the coasts, salt water intrusion may affect the flavor of your coffee. In this case, you may need to use bottled water or a more involved filtration system; but don't assume that the more expensive the filter or purification system, the better. Reverse osmosis filters,

A vintage coffee card from Woolson Spice Company,
the makers of Lion Coffee

for example, can strip your water of too many minerals, causing it (and your coffee) to taste flat. (Some tap water is so bad that it must first be treated with reverse osmosis and then have some minerals added back to it—but only the most conscientious coffeehouses and restaurants will go to such lengths.) Additionally, water softening systems can add excess salinity to your water, which will also dull the taste of your coffee.

One sure sign that you need to improve the water you use for brewing is if you find that the coffee you make at home tastes especially dull and flat. If this is so, seek the advice of the manager or owner of a good coffeehouse in your area; he or she will likely know a lot about any problems in your community's water and be able to tell you how to correct them.

Brewing Methods from A to V

There are several different methods of brewing coffee. Some produce a very specific flavor profile no matter what the coffee used. Turkish coffee and espresso methods are two such examples, producing a very specific taste, flavor, and tactile experience. Other methods of brewing merely emphasize a specific set of flavor components over others. Kevin Knox and Julie Huffaker, in their excellent book, *Coffee Basics,* recommend that more acidic coffees be brewed using a method with a higher degree of filtration, such as one using a paper filter. They also believe that more heavy-bodied coffees are best experienced brewed with a method like the French press, so all the body makes it to the cup (and hence to the palate).

Brewing choice comes down to convenience and personal rhythms as well as personal taste. People with limited time or who are on strict schedules may find that a programmable automatic drip brewer, which will have their coffee ready as they are charging out the door, is the best way to go. People with less predictable schedules may only want to make sure that when they're ready for a cup of coffee, they've got the beans to grind and water to boil. (This is far preferable to having coffee that was automatically brewed hours earlier, or to using beans that were ground the night before.)

THE STRENGTH OF COFFEE

Coffee should be brewed at a ratio of four ounces of ground coffee for every sixty-four fluid ounces of water; it is best brewed for four to six minutes through a drip filter; the ideal temperature range for brewing is approximately 195° to 205°F. These guidelines for brewing coffee were not arrived at lightly. The Coffee Brewing Institute was established in 1952 by both the Pan American Coffee Bureau and the National Coffee Association in order to scientifically study the process of brewing coffee. Under the direction of Dr. E. E. Lockhart, the institute researched what happens during the brewing process. By surveying thousands of people throughout the country, Dr. Lockhart's research also determined which methods of brewing yielded the cup of coffee people preferred most. The institute was disbanded in 1964, but Dr. Lockhart's research and brewing recommendations are still valid today—though they are widely ignored by all but a few equipment manufacturers and food-service operators.

Per capita consumption of coffee in the U.S. peaked in 1962. Since then, Americans have drunk less coffee, and drunk it weaker, despite all of the recent hullabaloo about a specialty coffee revolution. Many in the industry argue that people drink less coffee *because* they drink it weaker and find it less enjoyable. So why *do* they drink it weaker?

A driving force behind the weakening of coffee was the advent of robusta coffees, which big roasters began adding to their blends in the late 1950s and early 1960s, thereby saving millions of dollars. Since the change in blends was gradual, consumers did not notice anything overt; they just slowly began to enjoy coffee less. As the percentage of robustas increased in the average cup of coffee, even die-hard coffee drinkers began to find that four ounces of this robusta-laden coffee was too much, and they started using less. (When confronted with good coffee brewed weakly, they find it insipid and go back to robustas or give up altogether.) Roasters, rather than view this as a liability, cheerfully announced (and do so even today) that you can use less of their coffee. What they don't point out is that with robustas and other lower-quality coffees you will *want* to use less. Many consumers, over the years, have even decided on none at all!

Still other people choose a brewing method based on the aesthetic appeal of the brewing device itself. If a beautiful vacuum pot will inspire someone to slow down for a minute and appreciate a great cup of coffee, who's to complain? Whatever method you end up using regularly, don't be surprised if one is not enough. You just may find yourself with a stable of brewers—some regular workhorses, and other, more unusual ones for special occasions.

Automatic Drip Machines

High-quality automatic drip machines are capable of making a good cup of coffee, but usually not at their advertised full capacity. There are two reasons why this is so. First, due to the electrical power ordinarily available, a full pot of water cannot be heated quickly enough to complete brewing an eight-cup pot of coffee in less than six minutes. Second, most brew baskets on home brewers are designed too small to hold sufficient grounds for a full pot. This makes it impossible to make an eight-cup pot with adequate strength. You are better off making smaller pots of coffee with the right amount of grounds, making sure not to use more water than will brew through the filter in four to six minutes. After brewing, make sure that the brewer has thoroughly wet all the grounds you've used. If not, you're probably trying to make more coffee than the brew basket can handle. Either paper or gold filters can be used with an automatic drip machine. Gold filters produce coffee reminiscent to that made in a French press, while paper filters produce a clearer brew. The beans should be ground to match the filter type.

It is important to carefully measure the ground coffee and water. Two tablespoons, or one standard coffee measure, of ground coffee to six ounces of water is a good starting point. (However, be aware that most "cup" measurements located on glass carafes of automatic drip coffeemakers are marked as five-ounce cups rather than six-ounce cups.) Also, remember that if you pour twenty-four ounces of water into the coffeemaker, you will not get twenty-four ounces of coffee. Some water (about 10 to 12 percent) will be absorbed into the grounds and never reach the carafe.

A common mistake made in using an automatic drip machine is leaving the brewed coffee on the machine's warming plate. Once coffee is brewed it should be drunk immediately or put into a heated thermos. Brewed coffee left on a burner will burn or "cook," causing overextraction.

Cone Filter Drip Method

The Melitta (or Filtropa) cone filter drip brewing method is an excellent way to brew coffee. It is convenient and portable, and, most importantly, you can maintain control over the water temperature and brewing time. With a paper filter, a fine grind should be used; with a gold filter, a medium-fine grind should be used. Place the paper filter in the cone and rinse it out with very hot or boiling water until the "papery" smell is gone. When boiling water to brew coffee for a Filtropa cone, be sure to use fresh, cold water, and after the water comes to a gentle boil, let the water stand for about ten seconds to ensure that the water is at the proper brewing temperature of 195 to 205°F. Then pour it through the grounds into the cup waiting below. Again, when brewing, take care to pour the water through the filter at such a rate that the entire brewing process is finished in four to six minutes. For more even extraction, stir the coffee as it brews. Although this may seem like the simplest method, the result is still a full-bodied, well-balanced cup of coffee.

Chemex Pots

Chemex pots are glass coffeepots shaped like an hourglass; they use a filtration method for brewing coffee. As with the cone-shaped filter, the advantage of the Chemex pot is the brewer's ability to control the temperature of the brewing water. There are two different styles of Chemex pots, one that requires "folded square" filters and another that requires "folded circle" filters. The popularity of these pots waned during the 1980s, but they seem to be staging a comeback. Nowadays, many specialty coffee stores carry them.

Generally, the Chemex system delivers a cup of greater clarity than other paper filter systems, due to the heavier paper it uses. It also filters the coffee more slowly, preventing underextraction or too quick a brew. The danger of overextraction exists, however, and you should take care not to prolong the pouring of the water. The thick filters also mean you should grind coffee slightly coarser than you would for other drip methods.

Cold-Water Concentrate

Filtron and Toddy sell brewing apparatuses that are designed to brew a cold-water concentrate. Using this method, you steep one pound of coarsely ground coffee in eight cups of cold water for ten to twenty hours in a holding tank that sits on top of a glass container. A thick filter fits into the bottom of the tank and filters the resulting concentrate into the container. The concentrate is stored in the refrigerator and added in the proportion of one ounce of concentrate to three ounces of hot water. Coffee brewed in this fashion tends to be mild, with many flavor components missing because of the cold brewing temperature. But some people swear by it.

Espresso Machines

(See Espresso Basics, page 86.)

Flip-Drip Pots

The three-chambered flip-drip pot was originally popular in the 1800s. As with the stovetop espresso maker, the bottom chamber heats the water, the middle chamber holds the ground coffee, and the top is a receiving receptacle. Flip-drip pots are placed on the stove; once the water is heated, the pot is flipped upside down. The heated water then drips over the coffee grounds. Coffee brewed in one of these can taste metallic, especially if the

Q & A

Q. Can a stove-top moka pot brew real espresso? What kind should I buy?

A. No, a stovetop moka pot cannot brew real espresso, but it certainly makes an interesting (and even good) cup of coffee. Chances are you'll see one at a garage sale one of these days, and if it is no more than $4 ($2 is more in line) you might consider taking it home. Just make sure the rubber gasket that seals the two halves together hasn't been damaged by being kept on the stove top at high heat long after the coffee has brewed and boiled away. Actually, a moka pot combined with a milk steamer is a perfectly adequate and very inexpensive alternative to the less expensive home espresso machines. (Milk steamers are essentially little pressure cookers with long stems coming out of them and adjustable valves that allow you to steam a small pitcher of milk.)

pot has not been cleaned properly. Aside from the romantic appeal of imagining you are in the Foreign Legion, there's no real reason to use one.

Stove-Top Espresso Makers

Despite their name, these coffeemakers do not make true espresso. Instead, they brew a strong, thick, rich cup of coffee that is best served in a demitasse cup. Also known as moka pots, stove-top espresso makers have three chambers. The bottom chamber is used to boil the water, the middle one contains the ground coffee, and the top chamber is the place the coffee brews into. Coffee placed in the middle chamber should be tamped lightly. Place the pot on the stove over medium heat. Steam and water will travel from the bottom chamber, through the ground coffee in the middle chamber, and up through a spout in the middle

A single-cup stove-top espresso maker, which brews directly into a demitasse cup

of the pot. A medium-fine grind, finer than the grind used for an automatic drip filter, but coarser than the grind used for a cone filter, works the best.

French Press or Plunger Pots

A French press or plunger pot makes excellent coffee, using steeping rather than filtration to brew the coffee. Heated water and coarsely ground coffee are mixed in a beaker or glass carafe and allowed to steep for two to five minutes. A wire mesh filter/plunger is then pressed down slowly through the water and grounds, isolating the grounds at the bottom of the beaker. Coffee made in a French press should be served immediately to avoid overextraction of grounds still in contact with the beverage. It will have more sediment than filtered coffee, but tends to capture coffee's subtle aromatic complexities more effectively than other brewing methods will. Additionally, it yields a cup with greater body and texture than any other method of brewing. Using a French

Q & A

Q. *Is the French press the best way to brew coffee?*

A. Many coffee aficionados say that the French press or plunger pot is the best way to brew coffee. They argue that the coarser, nonpaper filter lets more aromatic oils and flavor constituents pass from the grounds into the cup—and they are right. The French press produces a thick, rich, heady cup of coffee. This is not to say that it provides the best coffee possible. That is more a matter of personal preference.

My personal preference (that is, the correct one) is for coffee brewed very strong, a few cups at a time, with a paper filter that has been thoroughly rinsed with boiling water. Simply place the filter in its cone over a coffee thermos and, before adding coffee, pour boiling water over the filter. Pour enough water through so that there is no papery smell to the filter. Then pour the water out of the thermos and put freshly ground coffee in the filter cone. Slowly pour boiling water over the grounds while stirring the grounds to make sure they all get wet. Pour slow enough so that the whole brewing process takes about four minutes. You'll get a cup that is unctuous, opaque, syrupy, and deeply aromatic—but without the gritty residue found in brew made with a French press.

press is also an elegant way to prepare coffee at the dining table. This style of brewing tends to be popular among professional coffee tasters because it is the brewing method most similar to the one used during cupping sessions (see page 17).

It should be noted, however, that recent research indicates that a certain class of substances called cafestols is found in any coffee not brewed with a paper filter. According to the same research, there is a very strong link between their regular consumption and elevated blood cholesterol levels.

Percolators

In a percolator, steam pressure is used to raise hot water up through a central tube to spray continuously over ground coffee held in a perforated basket. Percolation is a method of brewing that is generally held in disrepute; percolators boil the water and coffee together, causing grossly overextracted coffee. Coarse-ground coffee is used for percolators. Some percolators are electric, others are stovetop, and all produce a bitter, tepid brew.

Turkish Method

Unlike all the other methods of brewing coffee, boiling the coffee is considered desirable in the Turkish (or Middle Eastern) method. The boil achieved, though, is a very gentle one, and is more the result of the interaction between the heated water and the very fine grounds than of serious overheating. The coffee is brewed in a pot called an ibrik, which sits directly on the stove or over a flame. The coffee should be ground so fine that it has the consistency of flour.

To brew, mix equal parts of coffee with cold water and sugar. Pay close attention to the size of the ibrik; you should always brew the amount of coffee the ibrik was designed to hold (thus, always brew two cups of coffee in a two-cup ibrik, four cups in a four-cup ibrik, and so forth). Next, stir the mixture while bringing it to a gentle boil. When the powder no longer sticks to the spoon, stop stirring. Watch the coffee closely. After the brew begins to bubble, foam should gradually rise up. As the foam rises and thickens, remove the ibrik from the heat. Tap the ibrik on the stove or counter in order to deflate the foam somewhat. Return the ibrik to the heat. The coffee should be brought to a foaming but very gentle boil a minimum of three times.

Turkish ibriks

Serve the coffee in demitasse cups, pouring the cups half full, one at a time. When all the cups are half full, begin again with the first cup and fill each to the top. This custom of pouring the coffee into the cups is done to ensure that the grounds are distributed evenly, and everyone receives some foam. The result is a thick, sweet coffee that is a taste experience all its own.

Vacuum Pots

Popular during the 1920s and 1930s, coffee brewed in a vacuum pot offers a compromise between the clarity of the brew from a paper filter and the flavor intensity of coffee from a French press. The two-chambered vacuum pot was actually the first fully developed filtration system. Until very recently, finding a vacuum pot was an extraordinarily difficult chore. Now, however, many specialty coffee retailers carry them. Used correctly and carefully, a vacuum pot can give you a nearly perfect cup of coffee. However, a few of the reasons this method is not commonly used should be noted: It is complicated, finicky, and may even be dangerous.

An ornate re-creation of one of the
first coffee brewing machines based on
the vacuum pot principle

The best vacuum pots have filter systems that use no paper; rather, a filter is formed between close-fitting (but not completely sealing) glass or metal parts. This "filter" allows brewed coffee (but almost no solid particles) to pass through. This high degree of filtration can be achieved because of the strong vacuum formed during brewing, and the forced filtration that it causes.

To make coffee using a vacuum filter, remove the upper bowl, insert the filter or filtration apparatus, and add the correct amount of coffee grounds. Coffee should be ground medium-fine—approximately the same grind you would use for an automatic drip filter. (It is especially important to grind the beans with a burr grinder when using a vacuum pot without a paper filter, because an even grind with no filter-clogging dust is essential.) Next, bring a measured amount of water to a boil in the lower bowl and remove from the heat. Insert the upper bowl tightly and return the pot to reduced heat. Water will rise into the upper bowl. Allow it to mix with the coffee for one to two minutes, stirring gently, and remove from the heat again. The brewed coffee will return to the lower bowl in about two minutes.

If the brew does not return to the lower bowl in a couple of minutes, you may need to start over. Leave the pot on the stove for a bit longer this time in order to generate a powerful enough vacuum. The danger here is that a glass pot may develop such a strong vacuum that the pot implodes, causing hot shards of glass to fly every which way. Although this is a rare occurrence, it can happen, particularly if the pot is exposed to even a drop of cold water during the brewing cycle.

Now

All about Espresso and Espresso Drinks

Espresso Basics

Espresso is coffee that's been brewed quickly under pressure. The pressure, nine atmospheres or about 132 pounds per square inch, allows for the quick brewing interval: fifteen to twenty-five seconds. The resulting drink is a liquid explosion of flavor with the consistency of maple syrup. A one-ounce shot of espresso, after all, is made from the same amount of ground coffee that is normally used to brew a six-ounce cup. Espresso is not meant to be sipped but to be drunk quickly while it is hot. Its true appreciation is in its aftertaste, which should be refreshing and sweet and should last for up to half an hour. The memory of an espresso is as important as the immediate experience of an espresso.

Rather than creating a balanced portrait of a coffee's character, the espresso method of brewing accentuates certain characteristics and mutes (or even eliminates) others. Like the work of a mad impressionist painter, a great shot of espresso delivers a biased and wildly exaggerated representation of coffee's flavor while revealing its essence in an entirely different and refreshing light.

A perfect cup of espresso is also beautiful to look at. It has a dark, reddish-brown layer of fine creamy foam, called crema, which covers its top. When you swirl the cup, the crema should slightly coat the sides of the cup but remain intact over the top of the espresso. Some say that the crema acts as a lid to preserve the coffee's aromatics, and others point out (correctly) that a good espresso is drunk too quickly for this to matter. The chief appeal of the crema is in its beauty and its creamy texture.

Espresso is not a different type of bean, contrary to a common belief. Espresso may be made from any type of coffee, provided it is ground correctly. The questions of the best coffee or blend of coffees to use when making an espresso and how they should be roasted are valid ones. They are questions that the world's espresso experts will all answer differently.

A perfect espresso shot with
a beautiful crema

EXTRACTION AND ITS EFFECT ON ESPRESSO

	UNDEREXTRACTION	PERFECT EXTRACTION	OVEREXTRACTION
Taste	Sharp bitterness	Sweet, sharp, but clear acidity; origin characteristics noticeable	Bitterness that makes you pucker; pungent; no discernible origin characteristics; acidity muted
Aroma	Toasty, bitter smell; smells of hot water more than coffee	Rich scent of ground coffee; origin characteristics discernible	Burnt coffee; bitter notes
Crema	Thin, pale yellow	Deep, dark, reddish-brown, some streaks of golden brown; very thick	Proper crema may be noticeable underneath streaks of white, whiteness in crema is a sure sign of over-extraction
Body	Thin, watery	Full, thick	Full when slightly overextracted; thin when grossly overextracted

Most espresso is made from a blend of coffees from different origins. That blend is often roasted dark enough so that the beans glisten with coffee oils. It is also generally believed that coffees with greater acidity, such as Kenyan or Guatemalan coffees, should be roasted especially dark to soften the highly acidic flavor profile the espresso method tends to deliver. Thus, many espresso blends are made from coffees that are roasted separately and then blended together. Even so, it is often interesting to make a cup of espresso from a single-origin coffee. A dark-roasted Kenyan coffee, for example, makes an unusual, if somewhat unbalanced, cup of espresso. It won't have a lot of body, but it will have the acidity of freshly squeezed lemons and the aromatic punch of a florist's greenhouse, with an unexpectedly sweet and long-lasting aftertaste.

Q & A

Q. *I would like to invest in an espresso machine, but I don't know where to start. How much do I have to spend to get a reasonably good one?*

A. First, ask yourself what you're really looking for in an espresso machine. If your tastes run to the popular "milk" drinks such as lattes and cappuccinos, all you really need is a machine that will steam milk. Many of the less expensive machines can steam milk adequately, but they don't have the wherewithal to brew espresso at nine atmospheres of pressure (the level of pressure more or less defining espresso brewing). If, however, your goal is to make and drink really great straight shots of espresso, then you'll need an industrial-strength machine, and those generally run $500 or more.

Making Great Espresso

Of all the ways of brewing coffee, the espresso method is the most demanding and the most dependent on the skill of the brewer. In all other methods of brewing coffee, the fineness of the grind, the temperature of the brewing water, and the length of time the water stays in contact with the ground coffee are either easy to control or automated. With an electric coffeemaker, for instance, the temperature of the water and the length of time the coffee stays in contact with the water are controlled by the coffeemaker itself. These three variables, which determine the extraction rate, are much harder to control with espresso.

In technical terms, the perfect extraction rate is approximately 19 percent of the ground coffee's dry weight. Obviously, you have to determine the correct extraction rate based on taste, sight, and smell rather than percentages. Overextraction and underextraction are the two chief dangers (see the chart on page 87), but there are other ways of sabotaging your espresso, including stale coffee, a machine set to the wrong temperature or pressure, and poor water. Certainly, there are challenges to brewing perfect espresso, but the rewards far outweigh the difficulty of learning how. The following four basic rules will help you to master the art of creating the perfect espresso.

IMPORTANT NOTE: Following are some tips for brewing espresso with a standard, commercial espresso machine, that is, one that can accommodate seven grams of coffee in the portafilter and brew an ounce of espresso in fifteen to twenty-five seconds with nine atmospheres of pressure. Although very few home espresso units are designed to do this, many of the principles outlined here still hold true. If you are unsure of your machine's capabilities, follow the manufacturer's instructions to avoid possible mishap.

1. Use freshly ground coffee.

2. Use the correct grind.

3. Measure the coffee carefully.

4. Pack the portafilter correctly.

The Importance of Grinding

The correct grind determines whether the water will flow through the coffee at the right speed. Too fine a grind will result in overextracted espresso because the water will stay in contact with the coffee for too long. Too coarse a grind will result in underextraction—the water will travel through the coffee too quickly, producing a weak result. The finely ground coffee that is used in an espresso machine loses its aromatic complexity quickly, so the less time that elapses between grinding the coffee and brewing it, the more you will capture of the coffee's subtleties. It's ideal if you choose the freshest, best-quality whole-bean coffee you can afford, then grind it right before you brew it.

The first thing you will need, then, to prepare a good shot of espresso is a good grinder. Make sure the grinder you use is designed to grind finely and consistently enough for espresso; an inexpensive rotary grinder will not do. Carefully follow the instructions for your grinder. If you don't grind your coffee at home, but instead have your local roaster-retailer do it for you, here are a few tips to keep in mind:

• Pump machines and thermal block machines, which have their own water tanks, generally require very fine grinds. If your machine is one of these, ask for a grind setting for a home espresso machine or a Melitta system.

DETERMINING THE GRIND IN BREWING

Adjusting the grind of coffee for an espresso machine is an art in itself. Every single machine seems to require its own grind. Good old-fashioned trial and error is the only way to find the right one for yours. In determining the degree of grind required for your espresso machine, bear in mind the importance of the amount of pressure you use when packing the portafilter. You must use the same amount of pressure each time. The following tips assume that you have packed the coffee with the proper pressure.

• Start with a fine grind. Meticulously follow your machine's instructions to pull a shot of espresso.

• Use a one-ounce shot glass, or a measuring cup with one-ounce increments, to measure the brewed espresso.

• While pulling the first shot of espresso, count to twenty-five. Stop the machine when you reach twenty-five seconds. Now measure the amount of brewed espresso. If you have one ounce of espresso after twenty-five seconds, the grind is correct. If you have more than one ounce after twenty-five seconds, the grind is too coarse and needs to be adjusted to a finer grind. If you have less than one ounce after twenty-five seconds, the grind is too fine and needs to be adjusted to a coarser grind.

• For espresso machines with boilers, which require you to add water to a reservoir before brewing the espresso, use a coarser grind. If your machine has a boiler, ask for a stove-top espresso grind setting.

• When trying to find the right setting for your espresso machine, let your roaster-retailer know. Many are very accommodating to finicky customers attempting to find the ideal grind. If they're not helpful, perhaps it's time to consider taking your business elsewhere!

• Have your roaster-retailer write down the grinder's numerical setting on your bag of coffee. In cases when you require a specific grind that may be different than the general setting, this will help you and your roaster-retailer find the correct setting again when you need more coffee.

• Realize that grinders at different roaster-retailers, and even grinders at different stores within the same company, may have different numerical settings for the same grind. That is to say, a certain espresso grind may be a "3" in one store and a "2" in another. If you go to different stores to buy your coffee, you should take this into account.

• If possible, buy only a quarter-pound of coffee at a time, both to ensure freshness and to minimize the amount of coffee that may be ground at the wrong setting. Many roaster-retailers will allow customers to return ground coffee that has been ground at the wrong setting, even if the wrong setting was the result of a customer's request. Don't be afraid to request an exchange for the correct grind. A good retailer would rather give away a free quarter-pound of coffee than have customers drink coffee that has been ground on the wrong setting.

Packing the Portafilter

A portafilter is the espresso machine's filter basket: the apparatus with a handle that holds the ground coffee to be brewed. In commercial units and some home models there are often two portafilters: a "single" with one spout and a seven-gram capacity, and a "double" with two spouts and a fourteen-gram capacity.

In order for espresso to brew correctly, the water must flow down evenly over the entire surface area of the densely packed coffee, so that all of the coffee packed in the portafilter will be brewed. If the coffee has not been packed with enough pressure, the water will flow through the center of the portafilter. The coffee along the edges of the portafilter will be underextracted and the coffee in the center will be overextracted, producing a bitter taste. On the other hand, packing the espresso too densely will prevent the water from passing through the coffee at all. Thus, careful, meticulous packing of the portafilter is well advised. The following instructions apply to commercial machines. If you have a noncommercial-grade home espresso machine, you are well-advised to err on the side of packing too lightly.

- Measure the coffee. There should be enough ground coffee in the portafilter basket so that in the middle it is piled slightly higher than the rim. Using a straightedge, level the coffee in the portafilter basket by sweeping it across the ground coffee. The portafilter should be completely full, and the top should be level. This ensures an even surface for packing the portafilter.

- Pack the coffee. Using the tamper, push down lightly on the coffee. You should create a two- to three-millimeter gap between the top of the packed espresso and the top rim of the portafilter basket.

- Lightly tap the bottom of the portafilter against the counter. This dislodges loose coffee that squeezes out from under the tamper during the initial pack and sticks to the inside wall of the portafilter basket.

- Pack the coffee again, this time using a bit more force. Start with approximately ten to fifteen pounds of pressure for home units and up to thirty pounds for commercial units. Adjust based on the brewed outcome. (You can use a bathroom scale to help you determine what ten to thirty pounds of force is. Place your hand on top of the scale and push downward to determine how much force or "push" you need to apply in order to create the requisite pressure.)

- As you release the tamper after packing the coffee, twist the tamper in a circular motion over the coffee. This facilitates a clean pack and a smooth surface for the water to hit.

Brewing the Espresso

The two most critical things to keep in mind when brewing espresso are one ounce and twenty-five seconds (or less). One ounce is the desired shot volume and twenty-five seconds is the ideal brewing cycle (the amount of time the water should remain in contact with the coffee).

Two 20-second espresso shots. The reddish-brown
crema has formed.

After you turn on the switch to begin brewing the
espresso, it should take a few seconds before you see
espresso emerging from the spout(s) of the portafilter.
During these initial few seconds, the brewing water is
working its way through the densely packed coffee. After
approximately five seconds, you should see the espresso
begin to flow very slowly from the spout of the portafilter. From five seconds until about fifteen seconds into
the brewing cycle, the espresso may drip rather than flow
continuously. The espresso should be dark and reddish
brown. From fifteen to twenty-two seconds the crema
should continuously develop and thicken. After twenty-
two seconds you may notice the espresso flowing a bit
more quickly. At this point you should pay close attention
to the color of the crema. The moment the crema turns a
light or golden brown color, the brewing cycle should be
stopped. These are signs that the brewing process is complete. At about twenty-five seconds, you should have
approximately one ounce of espresso per shot. Prolong-
ing the brewing cycle will only cause the espresso to
progress toward a thin, watery, and bitter brew.

Talk Like a Barista

Barista The espresso machine operator, one who is fully informed and practiced (hopefully) in the art of coffee preparation; means "bartender" in Italian.

Caffè Americano Espresso diluted with hot water; one shot of espresso with up to seven ounces of water.

Café au Lait Half drip-brewed coffee and half steamed milk.

Caffè Brevè A latte made with half-and-half instead of milk.

Caffè Coretto An espresso "corrected" with the addition of liquor, typically brandy or a liqueur.

Caffè Latte Espresso with steamed milk and a thin layer of foam on the top.

Caffè Mocha Espresso mixed with chocolate and steamed milk and topped with steamed milk or whipped cream.

Cappuccino Espresso topped (or "hooded," like the Capuchin monks) with foam.

Con Panna With whipped cream.

Crema The reddish-brown, creamy layer of foam that sits on top of a well-drawn espresso.

Depth Charge A cup of coffee with a shot of espresso. (See also **Red Eye.**)

Doppio A double shot of espresso.

Draw To prepare an espresso shot. (See also **Pull.**)

Drip Short for drip-brewed coffee.

Dry Cappuccino A cappuccino with foam only, no steamed milk.

Espresso Pitcher A small, three- to five-ounce pitcher that the barista brews espresso into.

Espresso Macchiato Espresso "marked" or "stained" by milk foam.

Flavored Espresso Drink An espresso drink with a flavored syrup added.

Flat No foam.

Grande A sixteen-ounce serving of coffee or espresso drink.

Granita A dessert of shaved, sweetened ice flavored with coffee or fruit juice.

Group An espresso machine's brewing chamber, comprising the group head and the portafilter.

Group Head The circular unit that forms the upper half of an espresso machine's brewing chamber and into which the barista places the portafilter.

Group Switch The button on the espresso machine that turns the group on and off.

Knockbox A container with a padded bar across the top for the barista to use to "knock" the brewed coffee grounds out of the portafilter.

Lungo A long shot of espresso, about one to two ounces per seven grams of coffee.

Misto See **Café au Lait.**

Mochaccino An American invention that features espresso mixed with chocolate and topped with more foam and less steamed milk than a caffè mocha.

One Percent An espresso drink made with milk that has 1 percent milk fat.

Packing (the portafilter) The process of filling the portafilter with coffee.

Portafilter A handled device with a brew basket at its end that fits into an espresso machine's group head.

Pull Used as a verb to describe the act of making espresso, as in "to pull a shot."

Purist A coffee aficionado who demands quality and shuns the use of flavored syrups and the practice of diluting espresso with copious quantities of milk; will only drink an espresso, a macchiato, or a cappuccino. Usually the least happy customer in today's marketing-driven specialty retail store.

Red Eye See **Depth Charge.**

Ristretto A shot of espresso that is cut off at fifteen to twenty seconds (when the crema turns light brown) yielding less than one ounce per seven grams of coffee; an aficionado's ambrosia.

Short An eight-ounce serving of coffee or espresso drink.

Short Shot or **Short Pull** See **Ristretto.**

Skinny An espresso drink made with nonfat milk.

Steam Wand The thin metal tube on an espresso machine connected to the boiler that heats milk and produces foam.

Straight Shot An espresso served without milk, steamed milk, or foam; the drink of true purists.

Tamping The action of packing the coffee into the portafilter with enough force to ensure the proper extraction.

Wet Cappuccino A cappuccino with foam and steamed milk; usually the espresso, foam, and steamed milk are in a 1:1:1 ratio.

With Legs A drink to go.

A TALE OF TWO CREMAS

The controversy over whether robusta beans should be used in espresso blends is ongoing, but it shouldn't be. The taste of robustas in espresso is easily detected in proportions of as little as 5 percent. There is supposedly one particular compound that makes robustas taste the way they do. This chemical is responsible for making robustas, and any coffee they are blended with, taste bad. Robustas' characteristic flavor, best described as a harsh and rubbery grassiness, can be softened through careful processing, but it never goes completely away.

The malefactors who argue for the use of robusta in espresso correctly point out that espresso made from robusta-blended coffee produces a long-lasting crema—the fine, foamy amalgamation of water and coffee oil that forms over the top of a properly brewed espresso. A robusta-induced crema, however, is not quite as finely foamed, and it has the added liability of contributing the taste of tires and battery acid to the espresso. The proponents of robusta-blended espresso further argue that a thick, rubbery crema preserves the aromatics in the espresso by preventing their escape while the coffee is sipped. (They forget that an espresso is not meant to be sipped, but drunk at once and savored in its aftertaste.) However, drinking a robusta-laden espresso all at once is unpleasant, after all, and it is easy to understand why someone drinking such a potation would prefer to choke it down milliliter by milliliter, perhaps over the course of a few days. It is difficult to imagine, therefore, why anyone would want the additional agony of preserving the aromatics of a drink that is barely tolerable to begin with. But the reader should be the judge: Try almost any imported espresso blend from Italy (except for Illy, which contains no robusta). Do you like it? If so, PUT THIS BOOK DOWN AND STEP AWAY FROM IT. The Coffee Police are on the way.

Espresso-Flavored Steamed Milk Drinks

First of all, some semantics: Steamed milk drinks flavored with espresso are wonderful, tasty drinks, but they are not coffee, and drinking them does not make you a specialty-coffee aficionado. (In fact, true specialty coffee cognoscenti are embarrassed to drink them and generally do so only in private!) The following information is included so that you will be able to make these delicious drinks for your coffee-challenged friends. If you end up enjoying one yourself now and then, who's to know?

The milk steaming process should heat the milk to 150°F, which certainly is warm, but cool enough for most people to begin gingerly sipping their beverage. (A burnt tongue is often the result of oversteaming.) Steaming milk does more than heat the milk—it adds body and changes the texture. When milk is steamed, the foam, or the air that has been added to the milk to give it its additional volume, is incorporated throughout the entire volume of milk. If the steamed milk is used right away, the foam will still be incorporated throughout the entire volume of the drink as well. Once the milk has been steamed, if it is allowed to sit, the foam will rise to the top. The longer the milk is allowed to sit, the "drier" the foam becomes, taking on an airy consistency reminiscent of meringue. For traditional Italian cappuccinos and macchiatos, the milk is not allowed to separate. In the new American classics, such as lattes and mochas, the milk is required to separate slightly before it is used. Because of this separation, these are considered "layered" drinks, with espresso at the bottom, steamed milk in the middle, and foam at the top.

Regardless of its size, the pitcher should only be filled to one-third of its capacity. Because the milk is heated up to 150°F, and the sides of the pitcher will get very hot, a handle is necessary to hold the pitcher. Stainless-steel pitchers work best. The following are some tips for steaming milk:

- Always "bleed" or "burp" the steam arm, turning it on for a couple of seconds and then off, before and after steaming the milk. This dislodges any milk that is caught in the steam arm from previous steaming.

- Place the tip of the steam arm just below the surface of the milk. Slowly turn on the steam. Place the hand that is not holding the handle of pitcher on the opposite side of the pitcher, in order to steady it.

- As soon as the steam is applied to the milk, watch for the milk to swirl, or form a whirlpool, at the surface. This is the most critical aspect of steaming milk, with the whirlpool serving as a visual clue that you're achieving the proper consistency. (The tip of the steam arm, in relation to its depth in the milk, determines whether a whirlpool forms.) Your ears will also provide clues. If you hear a high-pitched noise, the tip of the steam arm may be too close to the bottom or the sides of the pitcher and no foam will form. If you hear a bubbling sound, then the tip of the steam arm is not far enough below the surface of the milk. The steam is not aerating the milk, and large, unstable bubbles with dry or airy foam will result.

• You'll know the milk is ready when the side of the pitcher becomes too hot to keep your hand on it. In order to preserve the best consistency of the steamed milk and to make sure the inside of the steam arm remains clean, turn the steam down to a gentle whisper as you remove the steam arm from the milk. The steam must be turned down (almost off) before the pitcher of milk is removed or milk will splatter everywhere. (And you'll never make that mistake again!)

• For lattes and mochas, the pitcher of milk should sit undisturbed for about ten to twenty seconds to allow some separation to occur. For cappuccinos and macchiatos, pour the milk immediately.

• For those who really want to get technical: Some kitchen or restaurant supply stores sell thermometers that clip inside milk steaming pitchers.

Classic Italian Espresso Drinks

These are the drinks that inspired a revolution in the way North Americans drink their coffee (and their milk). These drinks are much more codified than the North American versions: There is less latitude in what constitutes cappuccino, for instance, than in what can be called a latte. Also, Italians have very specific ideas about when and how often to drink these drinks, and who should drink them. When in doubt, you can never go wrong with a plain old espresso, the preferred beverage of "serious" people (not just coffee drinkers).

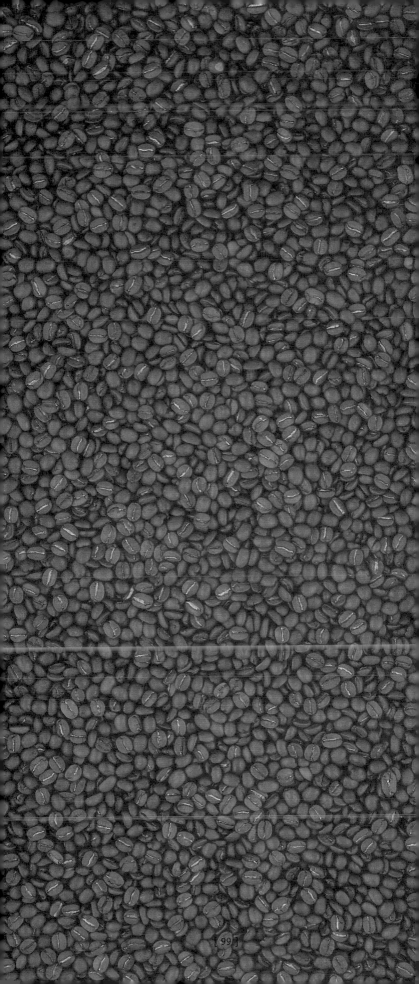

Cappuccino

The traditional Italian cappuccino is generally much stronger than the Americanized version, with the proportion of espresso to cappuccino foam much greater. Traditionally, cappuccinos are served only in the morning and not drunk throughout the day or after dinner, as has become the norm in America today. In cappuccinos, the espresso is always served at the bottom of the cup, with foam placed over the top. Cappuccino cups are wide and round, usually with a six- to eight-ounce capacity: Both single and double cappuccinos are served in these cups. The wide shape of the cup allows the foam to cover more of the surface area of the espresso than a narrow cup would; so when you sip a cappuccino, the espresso slides underneath the cappuccino foam and you get an equal taste of both. Cappuccinos are best enjoyed before the foam sits too long and layering occurs. When you look at a cappuccino served in the traditional wide-rimmed cup, you should see a brown rim of espresso lining the edge of the cup.

Cappuccino foam should be thick, rich, soupy, and have an almost silky texture to it. It shouldn't be dry or overly airy, nor should it have any large bubbles. The surface of the milk should almost seem to shine. Getting the consistency of cappuccino foam right can be tricky. If you're able to sip the coffee and the foam from the cup without having to use a spoon to scoop away the foam, then the cappuccino is just right.

This question "Wet or dry?" refers to the amount of hot milk you want to go along with the cappuccino foam. The most commonly used formula for the American "wet" cappuccino is one third espresso, one third cappuccino foam, and one third steamed milk. However, with the popularity of eight-, twelve-, and even sixteen- and the unnatural twenty-ounce cups, the proportions tend to get a bit skewed (as if these livestock-portioned sizes weren't skewed enough to begin with).

Espresso Macchiato

The espresso macchiato is a shot of espresso that is "marked" or "stained" with steamed milk. The espresso should be drawn directly into the cup in which it's being served. Just a touch of the foam from the top of some steamed milk is then spooned on top of the espresso.

A cappuccino (top) and a mocha (bottom), in traditional, wide cappuccino cups

When looking at an espresso macchiato from the top, you should see a brown rim of espresso lining the edges of the cup with a slightly domed dollop of foam floating in the center. The taste of an espresso macchiato is the taste of espresso smoothed out by just a bit of creamy steamed milk.

New American Espresso Drinks

Perhaps what best distinguishes the American culinary tradition is our ability to put a unique twist and an American stamp on old-world culinary traditions. This certainly has been the case with espresso drinks. The caffè latte and the caffè mocha are the new American classics. Most Americans consider lattes and mochas, and not espressos and cappuccinos, the quintessential espresso drinks: Sales trends at most coffeehouses and retail coffee stores reflect that sentiment. Ten years ago, who would have thought that when someone said, "Let's go get coffee," they would mean, "Let's go get a latte or mocha"? Coffee aficionados shudder at the thought of someone adding chocolate or sixteen ounces of milk to their espresso. But the merit of the new American classics is not in their purity but in their ability to soothe and comfort as well as invigorate.

Caffè Latte

The caffè latte is certainly the economic backbone of the specialty coffee industry, but it may also be the soul of the new American coffee culture. In most coffeehouses and retail coffee stores you will generally find one shot of espresso for every seven ounces of steamed milk. Thus, in an eight- to twelve-ounce latte you will normally find one shot of espresso, and in a sixteen-ounce latte, two shots.

The latte, perhaps even more than the martini, is open to personal customization. Nevertheless, the building blocks of a great latte are still well-prepared steamed milk and properly drawn espresso. The steamed milk, like cappuccino foam, should have more body than hot milk, especially during the first few sips before the foam and the milk separate. The texture of the steamed milk should be similar to that of cappuccino foam, but less airy. While cappuccino foam should taste like milky foam, the steamed milk in a latte should taste like frothy or foamy milk. The espresso should impart a rich, distinct flavor but never be bitter.

Other ingredients can be added to complement the taste of caffè lattes. Chocolate, cinnamon, and nutmeg are often sprinkled on top. Flavored syrups, which come

**Although the beverages are different, the allure of
the European café culture is undeniable.**

in dozens of varieties, may be mixed into the steamed
milk and espresso when the latte is made (vanilla,
caramel, mint, and almond are just a few popular flavors).

Caffè Mocha

The term "mocha" originally referred to coffee that
was grown on the Arabian peninsula and shipped from
the Yemeni port of Mocha. The history of this word's use
is fairly muddled. It is likely that most Europeans tasted
coffee before chocolate. Therefore, when chocolate first
appeared from the Western Hemisphere, they found it
reminiscent of, or confused it with, the wild and fruity
flavors of Yemeni coffee. Since then, the word "mocha"
has come to mean many things, including the flavor combination of coffee and chocolate, while it is still used to
describe coffee from Yemen (or even coffee from Ethiopia
that tastes like coffee from Yemen).

ESPRESSO RISTRETTO

In pulling a shot of espresso, twenty-five seconds is the usual and officially recommended time. This is because a serving of espresso of less than one ounce seems an alarmingly small portion to all but the most sophisticated espresso aficionado. Most coffee bars would rather serve one ounce (or more) than try to explain that a smaller serving (a fifteen- to twenty-second shot) of espresso is often much better tasting. This smaller serving is known in Italy and in many U.S. coffeehouses as an espresso ristretto, but it is often referred to as a "short shot." It is a sweet and aromatic coffee, and the best example of the principle "less is more" that you're likely to come across. Even in steamed milk drinks, you will find that your drink will be vastly improved by making or requesting ristretto shots.

Caffè mocha is made by mixing chocolate (either sweetened, ground chocolate or chocolate syrup) with espresso. Steamed milk is then added to the mixture. Most recipes specifically suggest that the espresso and chocolate be mixed before the steamed milk is added, in order to preserve the proper consistency and texture of the milk and to ensure that the mocha has a frothy, rich texture. As with the latte, the quality and taste of the espresso matter a great deal.

Caffè Americano

During World War I, American soldiers were not accustomed to the intensity of Italian coffee (which had not yet quite evolved into true espresso but was nonetheless strong stuff). Copious quantities of hot water were added to the strong coffee in order to approximate the taste to which American soldiers were accustomed. Particularly popular in the Pacific Northwest, the caffè americano of today is espresso with hot water. In most cases, around seven ounces of hot water are added for every shot of espresso. The americano allows the coffee drinker to slowly savor the coffee, and takes the edge off the intensity of straight espresso. While different in taste from drip-brewed coffee, it can be a way of guaranteeing you'll get a fresh cup in a restaurant or coffeehouse where you suspect their regular coffee may not be fresh.

A perfectly poured café au lait

Café au Lait

Traditionally, the café au lait was half scalded milk and half regularly brewed coffee—each poured simultaneously into the cup. In North America the term has come to mean many other things as well, including a drink made from half regularly brewed coffee and half steamed milk, with very little foam. Usually, the steamed milk is poured into the cup, mug, glass, or bowl first, which allows the coffee to mix more thoroughly with the milk.

Wow!

Cooking with Coffee

"That Heavenly Coffee" as an Ingredient

Coffee has been used as a flavoring agent in sweets, from breakfast specialties to late-night snacks, almost since the discovery of the roasted bean. Breads, cakes, muffins, cookies, candies, and all forms of sweet delights benefit from coffee flavor. But there is also a tradition of using coffee as a flavoring in savory foods: It can enrich and add interest to barbecue sauces and glazes for meats, chili beans and baked beans, and even pot roast and gravy. And coffee can add an intriguing dimension to cocktails.

In this book, we chose recipes that will not only accompany coffee—there are myriad of those readily available—but that actually include coffee in the ingredients. These recipes proved much more difficult to find, test, and develop into delicious, fool-proof formulas—and here's why.

The flavor of coffee is a result of the combination of the hundreds of chemical compounds that coffee contains (unlike, for instance, the singular flavor of raspberries). Adding coffee to a recipe, then, adds complexity, but it does not necessarily add a flavor component that is immediately identifiable as coffee. What it does add is an inscrutable richness and subtlety to certain foods.

As a cooking ingredient, coffee should be used carefully, so here are some general guidelines for you to follow:

- Consider using decaffeinated coffee in nighttime concoctions. (Or that extra helping of dessert may keep you and your guests from a good night's sleep!)

- In all recipes that call for ground coffee, grind it fresh, following the instructions as to the appropriate grind.

- In all recipes that call for brewed coffee, brew it fresh and strong, using a rinsed paper filter in a simple cone coffee maker and freshly boiled water. In most cases, make it at least twice as strong as you normally would.

- If you don't have a home espresso machine, consider getting espresso from your local coffeehouse. Take it home promptly (again, freshness is important) and use it immediately. The same goes for other coffees, too.

- If you cannot obtain freshly brewed espresso, try brewing espresso, French roast, or other dark-roasted coffee at triple strength.

- When using instant coffee in a recipe, remember that it is at least three times the strength of regular coffee, ground to a fine powder. Although we do not recommend drinking it, it is useful in recipes that would be affected by the excess liquid of brewed coffee or the insoluble grounds of coffee beans.

- Add coffee to any savory dish after all the other ingredients have been cooked. Otherwise, you may end up with a dish tainted by acrid, burnt coffee undertones. Coffee does not take well to long exposure at high temperatures.

- If you want to try adding coffee to a recipe that does not call for it, consider whether the dish will benefit from the color and depth of flavor that coffee will add. A delicately flavored scallop soufflé, for instance, would not likely be improved with the addition of coffee.

NOTES ON INGREDIENTS: All eggs called for are large. All flour called for is all-purpose, unless otherwise indicated. All sugar called for is granulated, unless otherwise indicated. Superfine sugar is a finer-textured granulated sugar that dissolves quickly in liquids. If you can't find it in your local grocery store, just put granulated sugar into a food processor fitted with a steel blade and process until fine.

WAKE UP AND SMELL THE COFFEE

Easy Banana Coffee Bread

MAKES 1 LOAF

This is a favorite childhood recipe for blender banana bread, brought up-to-date with a bit of coffee flavoring. Use a medium-roast coffee such as a Kenyan coffee, which has a fruity, clean, and distinctive taste that complements the bananas and nuts.

- $1^3/_4$ cups flour
- $^3/_4$ teaspoon baking soda
- $1^1/_4$ teaspoons cream of tartar
- $^1/_2$ teaspoon salt
- $^1/_2$ cup roughly chopped walnuts, preferably black walnuts
- 2 teaspoons very finely ground (powdered) coffee
- $^1/_3$ cup butter, softened
- 2 eggs
- 2 very ripe bananas
- $^2/_3$ cup sugar

Preheat the oven to 350°. Grease and flour a 9 x 5-inch loaf pan, knocking out any excess flour.

Sift the flour, baking soda, cream of tartar, and salt into a medium bowl. Add the nuts and coffee and stir to mix well. Place the butter, eggs, bananas, and sugar in a blender and blend until smooth. Add the banana mixture to the flour mixture and mix until thoroughly blended. Pour the batter into the prepared loaf pan and bake for 1 hour or until a cake tester comes out clean. Cool the bread in the pan, then store tightly wrapped in plastic wrap.

Coffee Crumb Coffee Cake

MAKES ONE 9-INCH CAKE

Enjoy a steaming-hot cup of coffee while you prepare this morning delight. When you take your first bite of this coffee cake, you'll get the crunch of the sweet, cinnamony topping. Then comes the surprise of a cake that's not too sweet, and flavored with coffee—a perfect accompaniment to your second cup.

- $^3/_4$ cup milk
- 1 tablespoon very finely ground (powdered) coffee
- 2 cups plus 3 tablespoons flour
- $^1/_2$ cup sugar
- 1 teaspoon baking powder
- 1 teaspoon baking soda
- $^1/_2$ teaspoon salt
- $^1/_4$ cup ($^1/_2$ stick) plus 2 tablespoons melted butter
- 2 eggs, beaten
- $^1/_3$ cup packed brown sugar
- $^1/_2$ teaspoon ground cinnamon
- $^1/_4$ teaspoon ground nutmeg
- $^1/_2$ cup chopped walnuts (optional)

Preheat the oven to 350°. Butter a 9-inch round pan or baking dish.

In a small saucepan over a low heat, scald the milk and immediately remove it from the heat. Stir in the coffee and set aside to cool.

Meanwhile, in a medium bowl, whisk together the 2 cups flour, sugar, baking powder, baking soda, and salt until well combined. With a wooden spoon, beat in the milk mixture and the $1/4$ cup melted butter until blended. Add the eggs and continue beating until smooth. Pour the batter into the prepared pan.

To make the topping, in a small bowl, combine the brown sugar, the remaining 3 tablespoons flour, cinnamon, nutmeg, and walnuts. With a fork, mix in the remaining 2 tablespoons melted butter until crumbly. Sprinkle over the batter. Bake for 30 to 35 minutes, or until a cake tester comes out clean.

Coffee Maple Syrup

MAKES ABOUT $2^1/4$ CUPS

Use this yummy coffee-laced syrup on French toast and you'll swoon! But, if you don't want to cause a scene, just pour it over spicy breakfast sausages, country ham, bacon, pancakes, or anything else that you think needs it.

$1^1/2$ **cups packed brown sugar**

$1/2$ **cup real maple syrup**

$1/2$ **cup water**

$1/4$ **cup ($1/2$ stick) butter**

2 teaspoons instant Italian espresso powder

$1/2$ **teaspoon vanilla**

In a small heavy saucepan over a medium-low heat, combine the brown sugar, maple syrup, water, and butter. Cook, stirring continuously, until the sugar is dissolved. Reduce the heat to low, stir in the coffee powder and vanilla, and simmer for 5 minutes. Serve warm. The syrup will keep, refrigerated, for up to 1 week.

Blackstrap Molasses Muffins

MAKES 12 TO 16 MUFFINS

This recipe turns out muffins that are rich and dark with the hearty flavors of coffee and molasses. They are perfect to wake up to or as an addition to a holiday dinner menu. A Colombian coffee would be a good choice here.

1½ cups whole-wheat flour

1 cup bran

2 teaspoons baking powder

Pinch salt

½ cup raisins

2 eggs

½ cup milk

½ cup honey

1 tablespoon finely ground coffee

¼ cup blackstrap molasses

¼ cup vegetable oil

Preheat the oven to 375°. Grease muffin tins or coat them with nonstick cooking spray.

In a large bowl, whisk together the flour, bran, baking powder, salt, and raisins until well combined. In a separate bowl, whisk together the eggs, milk, honey, coffee, molasses, and oil until blended. Fold the wet ingredients into the dry ingredients just until the dry ingredients are moistened. (The batter will be lumpy.)

Spoon the batter into the prepared muffin tins. Bake for 20 to 25 minutes, or until a cake tester comes out clean. Immediately turn the muffins out of the tins and let cool on a wire rack.

Blackstrap Molasses Muffin; ham and bacon with Coffee Maple Syrup (page 113)

Nᵒ4 And now this eager, hungry little group,
   Around the family table take their places;
It is not the meat, nor is it the soup,
   That brightens up their youthful smiling faces,
But 'tis the fragrance steaming from the pot,
Scull's Champion Coffee, fresh, and piping hot.

SNACKS AND SWEETS

Cappuccino Coffee Kisses

MAKES ABOUT 4 DOZEN

These meringue cookies are light as cappuccino foam—a guilty pleasure with no guilt. If you prefer a powdery dry cookie that melts in your mouth, rather than a cookie with a chewy center, turn off the oven after baking and leave them, with the door closed, for half an hour.

- $1/2$ cup (about 4 large) egg whites, at room temperature
- $1/8$ teaspoon salt
- $1/8$ teaspoon cream of tartar
- $3/4$ cup superfine sugar
- 1 teaspoon instant Italian espresso powder

Preheat the oven to 275°.

In a large bowl, beat the egg whites, salt, and cream of tartar with an electric beater at a low speed until frothy. Increase the speed to high and beat the whites until they hold a soft peak. Slowly add the sugar, a little at a time, beating until the meringue is stiff and glossy. Add the espresso powder about halfway through, so that it dissolves into the meringue.

Spoon tablespoons of the meringue, 2 inches apart, onto baking sheets lined with parchment paper. (Or, using a pastry bag fitted with a medium star tip, pipe the meringue onto the baking sheets.) Bake for 30 minutes, or until lightly colored and firm to the touch. Keep the cookies on the sheets of parchment paper, and transfer them to racks to cool. Peel the parchment away from the cooled cookies. Store the cookies in an airtight container.

Cappuccino Coffee Kisses; Chocolate Espresso Cookies (page 118); and a Kahlúa Coffee Truffle (page 120)

Brown Sugar and Coffee Fudge

MAKES ABOUT 1¹/₄ POUNDS

This fudge tastes totally different from the kind you are probably familiar with. Caramelly and coffee-laced, it can be addictive. Using a candy thermometer makes the job a lot easier (and you'll need the help when you are filling all the requests for more of this wonderful fudge).

- 2 cups packed brown sugar
- ³/₄ cup milk
- ¹/₄ cup (¹/₂ stick) unsalted butter
- ¹/₈ teaspoon salt
- 2 tablespoons instant Italian espresso powder
- 1 teaspoon vanilla
- 1 cup chopped pecans

Line the sides and bottom of an 8 x 8-inch pan with aluminum foil. Butter the foil and set aside.

In a medium saucepan over a low heat, combine the brown sugar, milk, butter, and salt. Stir until the sugar is dissolved. Increase the heat to medium and bring to a boil. Boil the mixture without stirring, until it reaches the soft ball stage (238° on a candy thermometer). Remove the pan from the heat to let the mixture cool (to about 110°).

Add the espresso powder and vanilla and beat vigorously with a wooden spoon, until the fudge loses its shine and begins to thicken. (This may take anywhere from 2 to 10 minutes.) Stir in the pecans and pour the fudge into the prepared pan. Cover the pan with plastic wrap and place in the refrigerator to set overnight. To serve, lift the fudge out of the pan, remove the foil, and cut into 1-inch squares.

Chocolate Espresso Cookies

MAKES ABOUT 4 DOZEN

Chewy and crispy, piquant and sweet, simple yet sophisti-
cated, these cookies can't make up their mind what they
are! But you will—they're delectable and disappearing.

2 cups flour

$1/_4$ cup unsweetened cocoa powder,
preferably Dutch process

2 tablespoons instant Italian espresso powder

Pinch salt

1 cup (2 sticks) butter

$1/_2$ cup sugar

2 teaspoons vanilla

1 cup chopped pecans

Powdered sugar for dusting

In a medium bowl, whisk together the flour, cocoa,
espresso powder, and salt until well combined. In
another medium bowl, beat the butter, sugar, and vanilla with an electric mixer set at medium speed until light
and fluffy. Add the flour mixture and beat until combined. Stir in the pecans. Cover and place the cookie
dough in the refrigerator for 2 hours.

Preheat the oven to 350°. Roll the dough into 1-inch
balls. Place the balls 1 inch apart on an ungreased baking sheet, pressing down on them slightly with your fin-
gertips. Bake for 12 to 15 minutes, or until the edges are
brown. Let the cookies cool on the baking sheet for 2 to
3 minutes before transferring them to a wire rack.
When completely cool, dust them with powdered sugar.

Coffee Cardamom Granita

MAKES 1 QUART

Since coffee's earliest days, cardamom has been used to flavor it, and it is still used extensively in the Middle East. It's a haunting combination, especially here, with the contrast of crystals of icy coffee and warm, spicy-sweet cardamom. Serve this treat as a pick-me-up on a hot summer day or even between dinner courses as a palate refresher.

$1/2$ **cup sugar**

$3/4$ **cup water**

3 cups freshly brewed strong coffee

$1/2$ **teaspoon ground cardamom**

In a small saucepan over a medium heat, stir the sugar and water together until the sugar dissolves. Increase the heat to medium-high and boil for 5 minutes. Remove from the heat and cool for 10 minutes. Stir in the hot coffee and cardamom. Refrigerate until well chilled.

Transfer the coffee mixture to a 9 x 13 x 2-inch metal pan (or metal bowl) and place it in the freezer. When the mixture begins to freeze around the edges (after about 30 minutes), stir with a fork, breaking up the ice crystals and mixing the frozen edges with the semi-frozen center. Repeat this mixing process every 30 minutes, for about 3 hours, or until the granita is consistently frozen throughout. Pack into an airtight container and store in the freezer for no more than 2 days.

Kahlúa Coffee Truffles

MAKES ABOUT 4 DOZEN

If visions of sugar plums dance in your head at night, these rich coffee-and-chocolate truffles will fulfill your dreams. They make a perfect ending to a special dinner party—that is, if you can resist eating them during the day! And don't skimp on the chocolate—using the very best quality is worth the expenditure.

16 ounces fine milk or dark chocolate

3 tablespoons superfine sugar

4 tablespoons unsalted butter

$1/_2$ cup crème fraîche or heavy cream

3 tablespoons Kahlúa or other coffee liqueur

1 teaspoon instant Italian espresso powder

$1/_2$ teaspoon vanilla

$1/_2$ cup unsweetened cocoa powder

Line the sides and bottom of an 8 x 8-inch pan with aluminum foil. Lightly butter the foil and set the pan aside.

In the top of a double boiler over simmering water, melt the chocolate, sugar, and butter. Stir in the crème fraîche until smooth and well blended. Stir in the Kahlúa. Remove from the heat, transfer the chocolate mixture to a small bowl, and cool.

Stir in the espresso powder and vanilla. Spread the truffle mixture into the prepared pan. Refrigerate for 4 hours or until firm.

Lift the truffle mixture from the pan and remove the foil. With cold hands, quickly form it into roughly shaped balls about 1 inch in diameter. Roll the truffles in the cocoa powder until well coated. Cover the truffles with plastic wrap and keep chilled until ready to serve. The truffles will keep, refrigerated, for a week.

Dark Chocolate Coffee Ice Cream

MAKES ABOUT 1 $^1/_2$ QUARTS

The secret of this ice cream is the long and meticulous whipping of the ingredients. Don't even think about shortcuts. Whip away, and it will end up like the most delicious homemade stuff that ever came out of a hand-cranked, ice-packed machine—only you don't need an ice cream maker! (You may switch the dark chocolate to milk chocolate, or even white chocolate. This recipe works with all three.)

- 2 cups heavy cream
- 1 tablespoon medium ground dark-roast coffee
- 10 ounces bittersweet chocolate, chopped
- 1 cup water
- $^3/_4$ cup sugar
- 6 egg yolks
- 1 teaspoon vanilla

In a small saucepan over a low heat, combine the cream and coffee. Remove from the heat and let steep for 5 minutes. Strain the coffee from the cream through a fine strainer. Let the cream cool.

In the top of a double boiler over barely simmering water, melt the chocolate. Remove the double boiler from the heat. Blend the water and sugar in a small heavy saucepan over a high heat. Bring just to a boil and cook 5 minutes, swirling the pan occasionally.

In a large bowl, combine the yolks and vanilla, beating with an electric mixer set at a high speed until light and fluffy, for 7 minutes. Slowly add the hot sugar syrup to the yolk mixture, beating continuously until thickened, for 10 minutes. Gradually beat in the melted chocolate and continue beating until cool, for 7 minutes.

Fold the cooled coffee cream thoroughly into the chocolate mixture. Place the ice cream in an airtight container and freeze until set, at least 5 hours, or overnight. Serve within 24 hours of making for the best texture.

Glazed Espresso Brownie Cake

MAKES ONE 8-INCH CAKE

This brownie has taken a step up in the world by becoming an espresso cake with a cloak of dark-chocolate glaze. (But it's still great with its humble sidekick, a big scoop of vanilla ice cream.)

CAKE

1 cup sugar

$^1/_4$ teaspoon salt

$^3/_4$ cup (1$^1/_2$ sticks) unsalted butter

1 teaspoon vanilla

4 ounces semisweet chocolate, chopped

1$^1/_2$ tablespoons finely ground dark-roast coffee

1 cup flour

3 eggs, beaten lightly

GLAZE

$^1/_4$ cup ($^1/_2$ stick) butter

3 ounces unsweetened chocolate, chopped

1 tablespoon honey

Preheat the oven to 350°. Butter an 8-inch round (or square) cake pan and cut parchment paper to line the bottom.

To prepare the cake, heat the sugar, salt, butter, vanilla, semisweet chocolate, and coffee, in the top of a double boiler set over simmering water, stirring until the chocolate is melted. Transfer the mixture to a large mixing bowl and let it cool for 10 minutes.

Add the flour and eggs and mix well. Pour the batter into the prepared pan. Bake for 30 minutes, or until a cake tester comes out clean. Set the pan on a rack and let the cake cool for 10 minutes. Turn the cake over onto a serving platter and remove the parchment paper. Let the cake cool completely before glazing.

To prepare the glaze, melt the butter, chocolate, and honey in the top of a double boiler set over simmering water. Remove from the heat and beat the glaze until it cools and begins to thicken. Pour the glaze over the cake. Let stand until the glaze is set.

SAVORY SELECTIONS

Coffee Lover's Barbecued Ribs

SERVES 4

Coffee adds depth to the high vibrancy of this barbecue sauce—it's like a brass band of flavors with the coffee playing the tuba! The ribs should end up delectable and tender, flecked with crispy bits of coffee-laced sauce. Serve them with plenty of hot french fries, a cold romaine salad, and your favorite dark beer.

- **4 pounds pork spareribs**
- **$^1/_2$ small onion, grated**
- **3 cloves garlic, finely minced**
- **$^1/_4$ cup packed brown sugar**
- **$^1/_4$ cup molasses**
- **$^1/_2$ cup catsup**
- **2 tablespoons red wine vinegar**
- **1 teaspoon Worcestershire sauce**
- **$^1/_4$ teaspoon Tabasco**
- **$^1/_2$ teaspoon freshly ground black pepper**
- **$^1/_2$ cup freshly brewed strong coffee**

Place the drained ribs in a large pan over a high heat and add enough cold water to cover. Bring the water to a boil. Reduce the heat to low and simmer for 1 hour.

Meanwhile, prepare the barbecue sauce. In a small saucepan over a low heat, stir together the onion, garlic, brown sugar, molasses, catsup, vinegar, Worcestershire sauce, Tabasco, and black pepper. Bring to a simmer and cook, stirring continuously, for 7 minutes. Remove from the heat and let cool slightly. Add the coffee and stir until well blended.

Place the drained ribs in a large bowl and pour the barbecue sauce over them. (You may leave the ribs in the sauce for several hours before finishing.) Finish cooking the ribs over a medium-hot grill, or in a 475° oven, for about 15 to 20 minutes, basting them often with the sauce.

Coffee Glaze for Country Ham

MAKES APPROXIMATELY 1¹/₂ CUPS

There's a famous (or should we say infamous) coffee gravy called "red-eye gravy," presumably because you'd have to be hungover to tolerate coffee boiled in a skillet with ham drippings. Herewith, we present a coffee-based glaze sparked up with apricot jam and brown sugar and mustard—everything a good ham sauce should contain. The bourbon lends a wonderful flavor, and since the alcohol is cooked away, it won't cause red-eye aftereffects, either.

1 cup packed brown sugar

¹/₂ cup bourbon or water

¹/₂ cup apricot jam

2 tablespoons apple cider vinegar

1 tablespoon Dijon mustard

1 teaspoon Worcestershire sauce

¹/₄ teaspoon ground cloves

¹/₈ teaspoon nutmeg

¹/₂ cup freshly brewed strong coffee

In a small heavy saucepan over a medium heat, combine the brown sugar, bourbon, apricot jam, vinegar, mustard, Worcestershire sauce, cloves, and nutmeg. Bring to a slow boil and cook for 7 minutes. Add the coffee and mix well. Use immediately or refrigerate up to several days.

Use the ham glaze to baste any fully cooked ham often, while it bakes. The glaze may also be used as a sauce for breakfast ham steaks or thick country bacon.

Black Bean and Sweet Pepper Chili

SERVES 8

In this zesty meatless chili, coffee adds a depth of flavor that accents the luscious dark taste of the black beans and roasted peppers. Serve garnished with grated Monterey jack or cheddar cheese, chopped green or white onions, chopped cilantro, and sour cream. (The chili tastes even better after a day's rest in the refrigerator. Reheat over a low heat until just simmering.)

1 pound (4 cups) dried black beans, rinsed well and soaked overnight

2 1/2 pounds red, yellow, and green sweet bell peppers

2 tablespoons oregano

2 tablespoons ground cumin

1 tablespoon ground coriander

1 tablespoon pasilla chile powder (or other dark red, mild chile powder)

1 tablespoon New Mexico chile powder (or other hot red chile powder)

3/4 teaspoon salt

1/4 cup olive oil

2 medium onions, chopped

2 cloves garlic, minced

1 (16-ounce) can crushed tomatoes in juice

1 cup freshly brewed strong coffee

Place the soaked black beans in a large pot over a high heat with enough water to cover them. Cover the pot and bring to a boil. Reduce the heat and cook until the beans are tender, 1 to 1 1/2 hours, adding more water if necessary. Strain the beans, reserving 2 cups of the cooking water. Return the beans to the pot and stir in the reserved cooking water.

Meanwhile, roast the peppers over a high gas flame until their skins are charred black. Alternatively, place the peppers on a baking sheet under a hot broiler and roast them, watching carefully and turning them as needed. Wrap them in a kitchen towel to sweat for 2 to 3 minutes. Slip off the skins. (You may have to rinse them quickly, but don't rinse away all the charred bits.)

Core and seed the peppers, and cut them into $^1/_2$-inch pieces, reserving all their juices. Set aside.

In a small sauté pan over a medium heat, toast the oregano, cumin, coriander, chile powders, and salt for 2 to 3 minutes, or until fragrant. Set aside.

Heat the olive oil in a large, heavy skillet over a medium-low heat until hot. Add the onions and garlic and sauté 3 to 4 minutes, or until transparent. Add the toasted spice mixture and cook an additional 5 minutes. Add the tomatoes and mix well.

Place the pot of black beans over a medium-low heat. Add the roasted sweet peppers and the tomato spice mixture and stir to mix well. Cover and cook for 20 to 30 minutes until the flavors have blended. Stir in the coffee and cook an additional 10 minutes.

Spice Crusted Lamb Chops with Red Onion Marmalade

SERVES 4

Seared in this spicy crust, mundane lamb chops become succulent and moist. The spice mixture is a balanced blend of sweet (fennel), savory (green peppercorns), hot (black peppercorns), and salty (coarse salt), made even richer with the addition of ground coffee. The red onion marmalade is the perfect sweet foil for the spicy lamb. Serve the chops with creamy garlic mashed potatoes, and pour a hearty zinfandel.

- 2 tablespoons fennel seeds
- 2 tablespoons freeze-dried green peppercorns
- 4 teaspoons black peppercorns
- 1 teaspoon coarse salt
- 4 teaspoons finely ground dark-roast coffee
- 8 (1- to 1$^1/_2$-inch-thick) lamb loin chops (about 2$^3/_4$ pounds), trimmed of excess fat
- 2 tablespoons unsalted butter
- Red Onion Marmalade (recipe follows)

To prepare the spice mixture, place the fennel and green and black peppercorns in a rotary blade grinder. Grind them briefly to a coarse powder, while holding the top of the grinder and shaking vigorously to evenly distribute the fennel and peppercorns. In a small bowl, mix the pepper mixture with the salt and coffee. Transfer to a plate. Coat each lamb chop in the spice mixture, pressing gently to make the mixture adhere. Shake off any excess. Set aside until ready to serve, for up to an hour.

To cook the lamb chops, heat the butter in a large heavy skillet over a medium heat. (You may have to use two skillets to fit all the chops without crowding, or cook in batches.) Depending on the thickness of the chops, cook them about 3 minutes per side for medium rare, or longer if desired. Serve with the red onion marmalade on the side.

Red Onion Marmalade

MAKES ABOUT 1 1/2 CUPS

1 tablespoon olive oil

2 medium red onions, quartered and thinly sliced

Juice of one orange

1/2 cup port

2 tablespoons balsamic vinegar

1 tablespoon honey

Pinch salt

Zest of one orange

Heat the olive oil in a medium saucepan over a medium heat until hot. Add the onions and sauté for 3 to 5 minutes, or until soft and just starting to brown. Add the orange juice, port, vinegar, honey, and salt, stirring well to combine. Reduce the heat to low, cover, and cook for 20 minutes. Remove the cover and continue cooking until most of the liquid has reduced to a syrupy consistency. Mix in the orange zest. Set aside to cool slightly. (The marmalade may be prepared and refrigerated up to several days in advance. Warm over a low heat before serving.)

Crispy Chicken Wings with a Quick Mole Sauce

A traditional mole sauce can take all day to prepare, but here it is broken down into a few easy steps. This is an appetizer, but you can also use the mole sauce to coat a whole roasted chicken for a really special dinner. By all means substitute 1 1/2 ounces Mexican chocolate, chopped into small pieces, for the cocoa powder. It will lend an authentic, although sweeter, flavor.

- 2 tablespoons sesame seeds, plus more for garnish
- 1/2 teaspoon coriander seeds
- 1/4 teaspoon anise seeds
- 3 whole cloves
- 1 (1-inch) piece of cinnamon stick
- 3 tablespoons New Mexico chile powder (or other hot red chile powder)
- 2 tablespoons unsweetened cocoa powder, preferably Dutch process
- 2 tablespoons brown sugar
- 3 tablespoons vegetable oil
- 1 large onion, chopped
- 3 garlic cloves, minced
- 1/4 cup raisins
- 1/2 cup sliced almonds, lightly toasted
- 1 stale corn tortilla or slice of stale bread, toasted and torn in pieces
- 1 (16-ounce) can crushed tomatoes in juice
- 1 1/2 cups chicken broth
- 1/2 cup freshly brewed strong coffee
- 3 to 3 1/2 pounds chicken wings, cut in half and tips discarded, if desired
- Salt and freshly ground black pepper to taste

To prepare the mole sauce, in a small heavy skillet over a medium heat, toast 2 tablespoons of the sesame seeds, the coriander seeds, anise seeds, cloves, and cinnamon stick until fragrant and turning dark, about 30 seconds to 1 minute. Let cool. Place the seed mixture in a rotary blade grinder. Grind to a powder, while holding the top of the grinder and shaking vigorously to evenly distribute seeds, cloves, and cinnamon. Transfer to a small bowl and stir in the chile powder, cocoa, and brown sugar.

Heat the oil in a large heavy skillet over a medium heat until hot. Add the onion and garlic and sauté until softened, about 3 minutes. Add the raisins and cook until plump. Add the spice and chile pepper mixture, stirring to mix well. Set aside to cool slightly.

Place the onion mixture, almonds, tortilla, and tomatoes in a blender and blend until very smooth. Pour into a medium saucepan over a medium-low heat. Stir in the chicken broth and simmer the mole sauce, stirring occasionally, for 15 to 20 minutes. It should be thick and smooth. Just before serving, stir in the coffee. (The mole sauce may be prepared and refrigerated for up to a day in advance. Warm over a low heat before serving.)

To prepare the chicken wings, preheat the oven to 400°. Rinse and pat the chicken wings dry, season with salt and pepper, and place in a large roasting pan. Bake them for 20 to 25 minutes, or until golden brown and crisp. Drain the chicken wings on brown paper to remove excess fat. To serve, place the chicken wings on a platter and pour the mole sauce over them. Garnish with toasted sesame seeds.

Old-Fashioned Pot Roast in Coffee Gravy

SERVES 6 TO 8

This is a simple roast made sublime by cooking in coffee. You won't be able to taste the coffee, per se, but its influence is felt in the finish. Be sure to serve with plenty of hot, buttered wide egg noodles.

$1/_2$ cup flour

$1/_2$ teaspoon salt

$1/_2$ teaspoon freshly ground black pepper

1 (4 to 5$1/_2$ pound) beef chuck roast, trimmed of excess fat

$1/_4$ cup vegetable oil

1 large onion, coarsely chopped

4 bay leaves

1 teaspoon dried thyme

2 cups water

2 cups freshly brewed coffee

1 tablespoon instant flour

2 tablespoons butter, chilled

$1/_4$ cup whiskey (optional)

Salt and freshly ground black pepper, to taste

Preheat the oven to 325°.

On a large plate or platter, stir together the flour, salt, and pepper. Dust the roast with the seasoned flour, discarding any excess. Heat the oil in a large, heavy ovenproof skillet over a medium heat until hot. Add the roast and cook on all sides until browned, about 5 minutes a side. Remove the roast from the skillet, leaving the drippings in the skillet, and set aside.

Add the onions to the skillet and sauté over a medium heat until they are softened. Return the roast to the skillet; add the bay leaves, thyme, water, and coffee. Bring to a simmer, stirring and turning to combine the seasonings with the roast. Cover and place the skillet into the oven. Bake for 3 to $3^{1}/_{2}$ hours or until fork tender. Remove the roast from the skillet, discard any bones or gristle, and set aside, loosely covered with aluminum foil.

To prepare the gravy, place the skillet over a medium heat, skim off any excess fat, and add more water, if necessary, to equal about $2^{1}/_{2}$ cups of liquid. Sprinkle the instant flour over the gravy in the skillet and cook about 5 minutes, stirring until smooth and thickened. Stir in the butter and the whiskey, if using, and season with salt and pepper. Return the roast to the skillet to warm in the gravy, then serve.

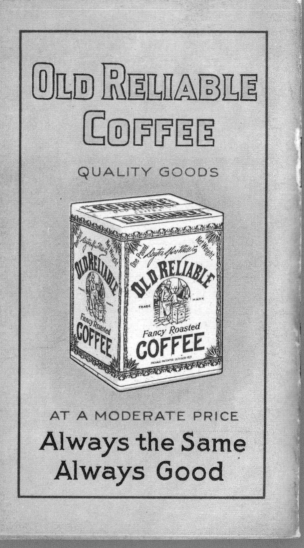

OLD RELIABLE COFFEE

QUALITY GOODS

AT A MODERATE PRICE

Always the Same Always Good

COFFEE COCKTAILS

Authentic Irish Coffee

SERVES 1

You don't have to be Irish or wait for St. Patrick's Day (or even bad weather) to enjoy Irish coffee. It's a soothing drink any time the mood strikes you.

1 jigger (1^1/$_2$ ounces) Irish whiskey

1 or 2 teaspoons sugar, or to taste

Freshly brewed strong coffee

Whipped cream

In a prewarmed 7-ounce stemmed goblet or coffee mug, combine the whiskey and sugar. Fill the goblet two-thirds full with hot coffee, stirring until the sugar is dissolved. Float a generous amount of whipped cream on top.

Coffee Libre

SERVES 2

Here's a twist on the Cuba Libre. The rum becomes imbued with the coffee and serves as a nice foil to the sweet cola. Substitute cognac or any good brandy for the rum and offer it warmed, without the cola, as an after-dinner cordial.

1 tablespoon freshly ground coffee

^{1}/$_2$ cup rum

2 cups cola

Pour boiling water through a paper coffee filter set in a coffee cone, letting the water drain through completely (this removes the papery taste from the filter). In a small saucepan over a low heat, warm the rum and coffee. Remove from the heat and let sit for about 5 minutes. Stir the rum mixture and pour it through the filter. Let cool. To serve, fill 2 tall glasses with ice. Divide the rum between the glasses and fill with the cola.

Café Alexandra

SERVES 2

This is a wonderful variation on the classic Brandy Alexander. We love it without the cream but go ahead and indulge if you want.

- **1 cup freshly brewed strong coffee**
- **2 jiggers (3 ounces) brandy**
- **2 jiggers (3 ounces) crème de cacao**
- **2 tablespoons heavy cream (optional)**

Stir together the hot coffee, brandy, and crème de cacao. To serve, fill 2 glasses with ice and divide the coffee drink between them. Stir in the cream, if using.

Caffé Almond Mocha

SERVES 2

Danger signs should accompany this drink—not because it's too strong, but because it can be addictive!

- 1 cup freshly brewed strong coffee
- $^1/_2$ cup Amaretto or other almond-flavored liqueur
- 2 tablespoons unsweetened cocoa, preferably Dutch process
- 1 tablespoon sugar
- $^1/_3$ cup milk
- Sweetened whipped cream

In a small saucepan over a low heat, stir together the hot coffee and liqueur. In a small bowl, whisk together the cocoa, sugar, and milk. Add the cocoa mixture to the coffee mixture and bring to a simmer. To serve, pour into warmed mugs and top with dollops of sweetened whipped cream.

Homemade Kahlúa

MAKES ABOUT 2 QUARTS

We have a friend who made gallons of this brew for Christmas presents one year. It would have been a frugal endeavor if she hadn't taken her eyes off the coffee and sugar, which boiled over and did major damage to her kitchen range. What she saved became delicious hundred-dollar bottles of Kahlúa, though!

- 4 cups sugar
- 2 cups freshly brewed extra-strength coffee
- 2 vanilla beans, split lengthwise
- 1 fifth ($3^1/_4$ cups) vodka

In a medium saucepan over a medium heat, combine the sugar, hot coffee, and vanilla beans, stirring until the sugar is dissolved. Bring just to a boil. Watch carefully and immediately remove from the heat. Stir in the vodka. Pour the Kahlúa into clean glass bottles. Seal tightly and let stand in a cool dark place for at least six weeks.

Café Brûlot

SERVES 10

This is a classic coffee drink that dates back to the turn of the last century. It can be prepared in an elegant chafing dish or in a simple double boiler. However you serve it, Café Brûlot is never out of style.

2 cinnamon sticks

10 whole cloves

Peel from 1 small orange, cut into thin strips,
     white pith removed

Peel from 1 small lemon, cut into thin strips,
     white pith removed

$1/_4$ cup plus 1 tablespoon superfine sugar

1 cup brandy

4 cups freshly brewed strong coffee

In the top of a chafing dish or double boiler set over simmering water, combine the cinnamon sticks, cloves, orange and lemon peels, sugar, and brandy. Warm this mixture, stirring until the sugar dissolves.

Spoon some of the brandy mixture into a ladle, and ignite the brandy in the ladle. Carefully pour the flaming brandy back into the chafing dish. When the flames have died down, slowly add the hot coffee. Stir until well combined. To serve, ladle into demitasse cups.

THURSDAY.

Dilworth's Coffee ✳

BECAUSE: ✳   IS UNEQUALED

No color poisoned, stained or damaged Coffees are ever used in its production.

It is composed of different varieties of selected Coffee, making a better drink than one variety alone.

It is thoroughly freed from dust and other impurities before it is roasted.

It is roasted and cooled by the most approved processes for preserving strength and full natural flavor.

It is then thoroughly screened, and freed from the chaff and films liberated by the roasting process.

It is packed in **Patent Air-Tight Packages** lined with waxed paper, which protects the Coffee from dampness and retains its full strength and aroma.

DELECTABLE CONCLUSIONS

Molten Mocha Cakes with Espresso Anglaise

SERVES 8

Serve these little cakes warm, so the surprise centers of melted mocha will ooze out onto the plates. For a dinner party, prepare these cakes a couple of hours in advance, keep them in the refrigerator until dinner, and bake them while you are eating your main course. Surround the cakes with Espresso Anglaise to finish this exquisite dessert.

8 ounces bittersweet chocolate, chopped

1 cup (2 sticks) butter

2 shots (2 ounces) freshly brewed espresso

4 eggs

4 egg yolks

$^1/_2$ cup sugar

2 tablespoons flour

Espresso Anglaise (recipe follows)

Preheat the oven to 450°. Generously butter and flour 8 small cake molds or soufflé dishes. Knock out any excess flour.

In the top of a double boiler set over simmering water, melt the chocolate and butter together. Stir in the espresso. Remove from the heat and set aside to cool slightly.

In a medium bowl, beat the eggs, egg yolks, and sugar with an electric mixer set at high speed until light and thick. Stir in the chocolate mixture and fold in the flour. Place the prepared dishes on a baking sheet. Pour the mocha batter into the molds, and bake for 7 minutes. The tops and sides of the cakes should be set, but the centers still quite runny.

To serve, invert the molds onto individual plates and let sit for about 15 seconds before unmolding. Spoon some Espresso Anglaise around each cake, and serve immediately.

Espresso Anglaise

MAKES ABOUT 3 CUPS

4 egg yolks

¹/₂ cup sugar

1 cup heavy cream

1 cup milk

¹/₂ vanilla bean, split in half lengthwise

1 tablespoon finely ground espresso

In a medium bowl, beat the egg yolks and sugar with an electric mixer set at high speed until pale yellow and almost fluffy.

In the top of a double boiler set over barely simmering water, heat the cream, milk, vanilla bean, and espresso until very hot. Discard the vanilla bean. Remove from the heat.

Slowly fold half of the hot cream into the egg mixture, then pour the egg mixture into the top of the double boiler, mixing well. Cook, whisking constantly, until the mixture is just beginning to thicken and coats the back of a spoon. (Be careful not to let the anglaise come to a boil or the eggs will curdle.)

Remove the anglaise from the heat and set the top half of the double boiler into a larger bowl of ice water. Stir often until the anglaise is cool. Strain any lumps from the anglaise. Cover tightly with plastic wrap and refrigerate until serving. Serve chilled or at room temperature.

Kentucky Bourbon Chiffon Pie

MAKES ONE 9-INCH PIE

Definitely an adult dessert, this one, with whiskey, cream, and coffee. You can also prepare just the bourbon chiffon, layer it with plain chocolate cookie crumbs in a stemmed goblet, and create an enticing parfait.

$1^1/_2$ cups chocolate wafer cookie crumbs, plus more for garnish

1 cup sugar

$^1/_4$ cup ($^1/_2$ stick) melted butter

2 envelopes unflavored gelatin

$^1/_2$ cup freshly brewed strong coffee

3 egg yolks, beaten

Pinch of salt

$^1/_4$ cup bourbon

3 egg whites

1 cup heavy cream, plus more for garnish

Preheat the oven to 350°. In a small bowl, combine the $1^1/_2$ cups cookie crumbs, $^1/_3$ cup of the sugar, and melted butter. Press this mixture into the bottom and up the sides of a 9-inch springform pan. Bake for 10 minutes. Let cool.

Soften the gelatin in the coffee for 5 minutes. Place $^1/_3$ cup of the sugar, the egg yolks, salt, and the softened gelatin and coffee into the top of a double boiler set over simmering water. Stirring constantly, heat the coffee mixture until the gelatin has melted and the yolks are starting to thicken, about 5 minutes. Stir in the bourbon. Remove from the heat and set aside to cool.

In a medium bowl, whip the egg whites with an electric mixer set at high speed until stiff. Fold the egg whites into the coffee-bourbon mixture until well combined. In another medium bowl, whip the 1 cup cream, slowly adding the remaining $^1/_3$ cup of sugar, until stiff. Carefully fold the whipped cream into the coffee-bourbon mixture.

Pour the mixture into the cookie crust and chill at least 3 hours. To serve, dust with the reserved cookie crumbs and garnish with additional whipped cream.

Classic Tiramisu

SERVES 8

This luscious dessert will draw raves from your family and friends. It is simple yet sophisticated—not too sweet and a perfect accompaniment to a great cup of espresso. Be sure to use a clear glass serving dish or bowl so you can see the layers.

  8 egg yolks

  1 cup superfine sugar

  1 cup Marsala wine

  1 pound mascarpone cheese

  $1^1/_2$ cups heavy cream

  2 ($3^1/_2$-ounce) packages ladyfingers, split in
      half lengthwise

  1 cup freshly brewed espresso, chilled

  $^1/_4$ cup unsweetened cocoa powder, preferably
      Dutch process

Place the egg yolks, sugar, and wine in the top of a double boiler set over simmering water. Cook, whisking constantly, until the mixture just begins to thicken and coats the back of a spoon. Remove from the heat and let cool.

In a medium bowl, with an electric mixer set at medium speed, whip the mascarpone cheese until creamy and light. Fold into the egg yolk mixture. In another medium bowl, whip the cream until stiff. Carefully fold it into the egg yolk and cheese mixture.

Line a 9 x 14-inch glass baking dish or large glass bowl with a single layer of the split ladyfingers. With a pastry brush, paint the ladyfingers with about $^1/_3$ cup of the espresso, just enough to moisten. Spread about one third of the cheese mixture over the ladyfingers. Sprinkle a dusting of cocoa powder over the cheese mixture. Repeat the layering with the remaining ladyfingers, espresso, cheese, and cocoa powder. Be sure to end with the cocoa powder. Chill, covered tightly in plastic wrap, for at least 2 hours or overnight.

Cappuccino Coffee Jelly with Cinnamon Whipped Cream

SERVES 6

This bears no resemblance to the artificially flavored gelatin dishes of childhood; it is infinitely better tasting. Clear jellied essence of espresso is topped with ethereal jellied foam, finished with a dollop of cinnamon whipped cream and chocolate-covered espresso beans (available at candy stores, coffee shops, and gourmet stores).

- 2 envelopes unflavored gelatin
- 3 1/2 cups freshly brewed espresso or extra strength coffee
- 1/2 cup sugar
- 1 cup heavy cream
- 1 tablespoon superfine sugar
- 1/4 teaspoon cinnamon
- Chocolate-covered espresso beans, for garnish

To make the espresso jelly, stir together the gelatin and 1/2 cup of the espresso in a small saucepan. Let the gelatin soften for 5 minutes. Heat the mixture over a very low heat, stirring until the gelatin is dissolved. Add the remaining espresso and the sugar. Stir until the sugar is dissolved. Remove from the heat and transfer to a medium bowl. Let cool.

Pour a generous 1/3 cup of the espresso jelly into each of 6 stemmed 8-ounce glasses and chill. Place the remaining espresso jelly (about 2 cups) in the refrigerator until almost jelled (the consistency of egg whites).

In a small bowl, beat the cream with an electric mixer set at high speed until it holds soft peaks. Divide in half and set aside. Beat the remaining chilled espresso jelly until it is pale and frothy. Fold half of the whipped cream into the espresso jelly. Spoon this mixture into the glasses. Refrigerate the remaining whipped cream. Chill for 2 hours, or until set.

To make the cinnamon whipped cream, beat the superfine sugar and cinnamon into the remaining half of the whipped cream. To serve, spoon dollops of the cinnamon whipped cream onto each jelly. Garnish with some chocolate-covered espresso beans.

Mousse au Café

SERVES 4 TO 6

This rich chocolate mousse is served in the traditional French family style, from a big bowl, dished up by the spoonful—big spoonfuls. Use the finest quality chocolate that you can afford—and the best espresso—for the very best results.

8 ounces bittersweet or dark chocolate, chopped

$1/2$ cup heavy cream

1 shot (1 ounce) freshly brewed espresso

3 egg yolks

5 egg whites

$1/4$ cup superfine sugar

Place the chocolate, cream, and espresso in a double boiler set over simmering water. Stir until melted and smooth. Remove from the heat and set aside to cool.

Transfer the cooled chocolate mixture into a large bowl. With an electric mixer set at medium speed, beat the egg yolks into the chocolate mixture, one at a time, until thoroughly combined. In a medium bowl, beat the egg whites with an electric mixer set at high speed, slowly adding the sugar, until stiff. Carefully fold the egg whites into the chocolate mixture. Spoon the mousse into a large decorative serving bowl. Cover with plastic wrap and refrigerate until well chilled for up to one day.

Old-Fashioned Chocolate Layer Cake

MAKES ONE 9-INCH CAKE

When you feel like the comfort of a good old-fashioned piece of chocolate cake with your cup of coffee, here it is. It has a deep, dark, rich flavor that is satisfying to the last crumb. And it's easy to make and richly deserving of a place in your "favorite recipes" file.

- 2 cups flour
- 1 cup unsweetened cocoa powder, preferably Dutch process
- 1 teaspoon baking powder
- 1 teaspoon baking soda
- 3/4 teaspoon salt
- 3 ounces semisweet chocolate, chopped into small pieces
- 1 cup freshly brewed extra strength coffee
- 3 eggs
- 1 1/2 cups sugar
- 1/2 cup (1 stick) unsalted butter, softened
- 1 teaspoon vanilla
- 1 cup buttermilk
- Fudgey Chocolate Frosting (recipe follows)

Preheat the oven to 350°. Grease and flour two 9-inch cake pans, knocking out any excess flour. Cut 2 rounds of parchment paper to line the bottoms of the cake pans.

In a medium mixing bowl, whisk together the flour, cocoa, baking powder, baking soda, and salt. In a small bowl, combine the chocolate and hot coffee, stirring until the chocolate is melted and smooth.

In a large bowl, beat the eggs, sugar, butter, and vanilla with an electric mixer set at high speed until light and fluffy. Add the coffee and chocolate mixture and blend. Add the flour mixture alternately with the buttermilk, mixing until well blended. Pour the batter into the prepared pans. Bake for 25 to 30 minutes or until a cake tester comes out clean.

Cool cakes on wire racks before removing them from the pans. When ready to frost, invert the cakes and peel off the parchment paper. Spread the frosting between layers, then frost the sides, and finish with the top of cake.

Fudgey Chocolate Frosting

FROSTS ONE 9-INCH LAYER CAKE

- 1¼ cups heavy cream
- 3 tablespoons sugar
- 3 tablespoons light corn syrup
- 1¼ pounds semisweet chocolate, chopped
- ¾ cup (1½ sticks) butter, cut in small pieces

Combine the cream, sugar, and corn syrup in a heavy saucepan over a medium heat. Cook, stirring continuously, just until the mixture comes to a boil. Immediately remove from the heat. Stir in the chocolate until smooth. Add the butter, piece by piece, blending thoroughly after each addition. Place the frosting in the refrigerator, if necessary, to thicken before spreading.

RESOURCES

After much debate, we've decided that with so many excellent coffee roasters, large and small, rural and urban, across the United States and beyond, we could not even begin to list them all, let alone give evaluations and endorsements. Usually, the best resource for questions about coffee and coffee equipment is your favorite roaster-retailer. However, for coffee aficionados who take an interest in the coffee journey less traveled, we offer the following. **Note:** There are (literally) hundreds of thousands of web sites dedicated to coffee. We suggest that you be as specific as possible in your searches in order to avoid a lot of false leads.

Brewing Equipment
Windward Northwest
P.O. Box 380
Clinton, WA 98326
(800) 215-3606

Windward is the American importer of the British Cona vacuum pots.

Flavor Seal Corporation
1780 Maple Street
Northfield, IL 60093
(708) 446-3550
Flavor Seal is the manufacturer of half-gallon stainless steel vacuum pots.

Boyd's Coffee Company
19730 NE Sandy Boulevard
P.O. Box 20547
Portland, OR 97220
(503) 666-4545; (800) 545-4077

This roaster sells the Dutch Technivorm line of home coffee brewers.

Beans and Machines
1121 1st Avenue
Seattle, WA 98101
(888) 625-1482
http://www.beansmachines.com

1st Line Equipment LLC
(888) 933-5947; Canada and international (201) 422-0474
http://www.1st-line.com

Both Beans and Machines and First Line are retailers and e-tailers—good sources for home espresso machines and an extensive line of brewers and brewing apparatuses. The Beans and Machines site includes a small section of used commercial equipment for the home.

HOME COFFEE ROASTING

The Coffee Project
P.O. Box 93941
Los Angeles, CA 90093
http://www.coffeeproject.com

Sweet Maria's Coffee Roastery
9 East 2nd Avenue
Columbus, OH 43201
http://www.sweetmarias.com

These two excellent sites offer all the equipment, information, and green beans you'll need. They've also fostered an online community of home roasters who exchange roasting tips.

GENERAL COFFEE RESOURCES

La Torcaza Estate
http://www.estatecoffee.com

Here's a unique, year-round look at all the steps of coffee production with images of the estate.

SWISS WATER® Decaffeinated Coffees
95 Moatfield Drive
Don Mills, ON M3B 3L6
Canada
(800) 667-6181
http://www.swisswater.com

This site is an excellent resource for decaffeinated coffee info, from where to purchase it to how decaffeination is done.

Coffee Science Source
15 Maiden Lane
New York, NY 10038
http://www.coffeescience.org

The CSS was created by the National Coffee Association to gather and disseminate the most up-to-date information on coffee, caffeine, and health.

Java Ventures
4104 24th Street Suite 421
San Francisco, CA 94114
(415) 824-1484
http://www.javaventures.com

If you wonder what it's like to be a coffee buyer or broker, traveling to remote coffee estates in exotic countries, you might consider a trip with Java Ventures.

Smithsonian Migratory Bird Institute
National Zoological Park
3100 Connecticut Avenue NW
Washington DC 20008
(202) 673-4800
http://www.si.edu/smbc

All the virtues of shade-grown coffee are extolled in this site.

Transfair USA
52 9th Street
Oakland, CA 94607
(510) 663-5260
http://www.transfairusa.org

For all the information on Fair Trade coffee, check out the Trans-Fair USA site.

The Coffee Review
http://www.coffeereview.com

When some of the industry's best palates gather for cupping sessions of coffees submitted from roasters throughout the country, the results are provided online here.

Tea and Coffee Trade Journal
130 42nd Street
New York, NY 10036
http://www.teacofmag.com

The coffee industry's preeminent trade magazine often writes on topics of interest to specialty coffee fanatics.

Specialty Coffee Association of America (SCAA)
One World Trade Center
Suite 1200
Long Beach, CA 90831-1200
(562) 624-4100
http://www.scaa.com

The SCAA is the coffee industry's resource for difficult-to-answer questions. They sell many coffee-related books and paraphernalia that may be of interest to both industry insider and consumer alike.

http://www.coffeeuniverse.com

http://www.caffeinearchive.com

To get lost in the cyber universe of coffee, check out either of these two sites and the extraordinary number of links each contains.

http://www.lucidcafe.com

This site is an excellent all-around resource, particularly for baristas and espresso aficionados.

If you would like to contact the authors you may write to:

Castle Communications
2118 Wilshire Blvd. #634
Santa Monica, CA 90403

or email

Timothy J. Castle:
qahwah@aol.com

Joan Nielsen:
joanielsen@aol.com

INDEX